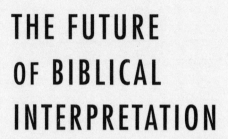

THE FUTURE
OF BIBLICAL
INTERPRETATION

RESPONSIBLE PLURALITY
IN BIBLICAL HERMENEUTICS

EDITED BY STANLEY E. PORTER
AND MATTHEW R. MALCOLM

IVP Academic
An imprint of InterVarsity Press
Downers Grove, Illinois

InterVarsity Press
P.O. Box 1400, Downers Grove, IL 60515-1426
Internet: www.ivpress.com
Email: email@ivpress.com

InterVarsity Press® is the book-publishing division of InterVarsity Christian Fellowship/USA®, a movement of students
and faculty active on campus at hundreds of universities, colleges and schools of nursing in the United States of
America, and a member movement of the International Fellowship of Evangelical Students. For information about
local and regional activities, write Public Relations Dept., InterVarsity Christian Fellowship/USA, 6400 Schroeder
Rd., P.O. Box 7895, Madison, WI 53707-7895, or visit the IVCF website at www.intervarsity.org.

Cover design: David Fassett
Interior design: Beth Hagenberg
Image: abstract background: ©Sergii Tsololo/iStockphoto

ISBN 978-0-8308-4041-0 (print)
ISBN 978-0-8308-7959-5 (digital)

Printed in the United States of America ∞

Library of Congress Cataloging-in-Publication Data
A catalog record for this book is available from the Library of Congress.

P	21	20	19	18	17	16	15	14	13	12	11	10	9	8	7	6	5	4	3	2	1
Y	30	29	28	27	26	25	24	23	22	21	20	19	18	17	16	15	14	13			

Contents

Introduction

Stanley E. Porter and Matthew R. Malcolm

THE TWENTY-FIRST CENTURY IS AN AGE in which religious conviction is sometimes considered a matter of private opinion, and sometimes considered a most public matter of life and death. Religious texts lead some to war, and others to peace. In such an environment, reflection on interpretation of religious texts is a crucially pressing issue. The Christian Bible, as the most published religious book in history, demands particular attention.

Beyond this, the Bible itself provocatively calls for the engagement of serious listeners. The New Testament book of Hebrews claims that "in these last days, [God] has spoken . . . by a Son" (Heb 1:2). Millions across the centuries have taken this claim seriously, and millions continue to today.

Yet these millions come from a variety of settings and make use of the Bible in a variety of ways. They find in the Bible a plurality of voices and reach a plurality of interpretations. Even within the Bible itself, one can discern a variety of interpretive approaches and results. If one were to ask the various writers of the New Testament what Psalm 8 means, or who is identified by the Servant of Isaiah, one would hear a variety of answers—not necessarily dissonant answers, but plural in number.

Some parts of the Bible, by their very genre, invite a plurality of interpretations (such as poetry or apocalyptic), while some parts resist it. But even the most open of texts cannot be *infinitely* open, or they would have no reason to exist. So how can readers of the Bible appropriately acknowledge and do justice to plurality, while being responsible as readers? The present book exists as a focused attempt to address this question. In short, it advocates a hermeneutically informed awareness of parameters within which responsibly productive readings will occur.

It is important from the outset to point out that even within this book, the reader will encounter a plurality of voices. It should not be thought that all the contributors wholeheartedly share the same philosophy of hermeneutics or approach to biblical interpretation. Nevertheless, they have kindly agreed to have their contributions appear within a singular project that carries, by its framing and arrangement, a certain overall concordance. That framing, of course, begins with this introduction.

Of fundamental importance to this project is the view of hermeneutics as a philosophy of human understanding. That is, hermeneutics is not a set of rules (human or otherwise) for the interpretation of texts, but an attempt to reflect at a more abstract level on how productive human understanding takes place. This perspective is a feature of the scholarly career of the first contributor, Anthony Thiselton, in whose honor these essays were first presented at a conference at the University of Nottingham. This conference was funded in part by the university, and we are grateful for this. Thiselton's contribution, "The Future of Biblical Interpretation and Responsible Plurality in Hermeneutics," therefore exhibits an interest in the significance of "openness," particularity and polyphony in human communication, as discussed in philosophical hermeneutics and exemplified in the Bible.

From this wide-ranging and suggestive survey of the topic, the volume moves to consider more precisely the role of theology in addressing the hermeneutical task, with Stanley Porter's contribution, "Biblical Hermeneutics and *Theological* Responsibility." Porter's essay offers definitions of hermeneutics and interpretation that are important to keep in mind throughout the rest of the volume. Significantly, he begins by considering hermeneutics itself (which has in fact been historically associated with understanding the Bible), before considering how one might exercise theological responsibility in this context. Rejecting "theological interpretation" as a means of exercising such responsibility, he urges an awareness of the complexity of the task that nevertheless attempts to bring "the two horizons of our theology—the original formulation as found in the text and the current understanding—into meaningful dialogue."

From this point, the volume may be read as applying such a theologically informed understanding of hermeneutics to the Bible, as canonical Christian Scripture. Richard Briggs's contribution, "Biblical Hermeneutics and *Scriptural* Responsibility," considers a number of ways in which Scripture might be construed by different readers or reading situations and offers a way forward in evaluating the readings that arise from such varying construals. He finishes by positively suggesting "some of the substantive theological/hermeneutical construals which . . . I think are of most significance in taking Christian Scripture responsibly."

Matthew Malcolm's contribution, "Biblical Hermeneutics and *Kerygmatic* Responsibility," may be read as continuing this trajectory. Accepting that interpretation of the Bible as Scripture ought to arise from a robust philosophy of general hermeneutics, Malcolm urges that such "arising" involves a figurative resurrection from the general hermeneutical grave, such that "Christian interpretation" of the Bible involves both continuity with general hermeneutics and the transcending recognition that Old and New Testaments bear witness to Jesus as risen Lord. It is only with such a perspective that readers may perceive "all that the prophets have declared" (Lk 24:25).

At this point the volume moves to consider what it means for such readers of the Bible to remain responsibly critical and able to engage with readers who do not share their "construal" of Scripture. Broadly, it would seem that most contributors to this volume would affirm the need to acknowledge contextualization, diachronic conversation across horizons, and the expectation of concordant polyphony. James Dunn's contribution, "Biblical Hermeneutics and *Historical* Responsibility," emphasizes the need to do justice to contextualization, especially in relation to the horizon of the text. Robert Morgan's contribution, "Biblical Hermeneutics and *Critical* Responsibility," appreciates the theological situatedness of the Christian historical-critical interpreter, thus offering a complementary emphasis on the horizon of the reader.

Having considered the orientation of Christian interpreters of Scripture toward those who might hold to alternative construals of the Bible, the volume then turns to consider how Christian interpreters are oriented to one another. Tom Greggs's contribution, "Biblical Hermeneutics and *Relational* Responsibility," presents a Protestant account of the authority of the creeds of the early ecumenical church councils for scriptural interpretation, seeing these as providing parameters of responsibility for those who would identify themselves as belonging to the church. Walter Moberly's contribution, "Biblical Hermeneutics and *Ecclesial* Responsibility," essentially advocates an approach to the Bible that is neither naively ecclesial (and so in denial of critical issues) nor naively critical (and so in denial of the situatedness of the interpreter).

The editors then conclude with a supportive critical response to these essays, identifying remaining hermeneutical issues.

This volume thus speaks with multiple voices from a plurality of subjects, each proposing a particular parameter of responsibility for productive interpretation of the Bible. The collection resists simple univocity, and yet, when viewed as a distinct volume as above, can be seen to exemplify the concordant polyphonic approach that it advocates. As such, it is our hope that it will prompt continuing discussion of these crucial issues.

1

The Future of Biblical Interpretation and Responsible Plurality in Hermeneutics

Anthony C. Thiselton

Aʟᴛʜᴏᴜɢʜ ᴘʟᴜʀᴀʟɪᴛʏ ɪɴ ɪɴᴛᴇʀᴘʀᴇᴛᴀᴛɪᴏɴ and the future of hermeneutics do overlap, it is not at all clear that the two subjects constitute the same issue. First I shall try to assess what "responsible plurality" might involve, by distinguishing between different *types* of plurality. Meanwhile I shall try to offer some possible assessments. One problem here, though, is that Mikhail Bakhtin, whose concept of polyphonic meaning I strongly support, dislikes the term *plurality*. Furthermore, in relation to the future of interpretation, he warns emphatically that genuine *creativity excludes* any notion of a clearly circumscribed or rigidly defined future, which we can easily determine or predict. In the final quarter, therefore, I shall attempt not to make predictions but to offer some comments on future possibilities and hopes in hermeneutics.

Gᴇɴʀᴇ: Sʏᴍʙᴏʟ, Pᴏᴇᴛʀʏ ᴀɴᴅ "Oᴘᴇɴ" Tᴇxᴛs

My first thesis may be inferred from my argument in *New Horizons in*

Hermeneutics.[1] I claim first that *responsible* plurality depends largely on *literary genre* and context. To begin with obvious examples, *symbolism* and *poetry* invite multiple levels of interpretation in a way that, for example, *historical report* would not. We have only to reflect on the book of Revelation. To quote Robert Gundry, "Symbolic language fills the Book of Revelation, as it fills other apocalyptic literature."[2] One example which he considers is the New Jerusalem in Rev 21:1–22:5. If we interpret this as a city, we find that each of its gates is pearl (Rev 21:21); its streets are transparent gold (Rev 21:18); and it is fifteen hundred miles not only in breadth and length, but also in height (Rev 21:16). It contains the tree of life, of which the leaves are for the "healing of the nations" (Rev 22:2).[3] Gundry concludes that the New Jerusalem is not a geographical location but denotes the people of God. George Caird compares with this the symbols in Ezekiel and in Daniel, especially Ezek 43:2 and Dan 7:9, commenting, "To compile a catalogue is to unweave the rainbow. . . . *This is not photographic art.* . . . [John's] aim is to set the echoes of memory and association ringing."[4]

This might seem obvious, almost to the point of banality. But two lessons emerge at once for hermeneutics. First, there is a tendency in so many studies of hermeneutics to *generalize* about problems of meaning, including whether meanings are one or many, or even whether biblical language is expressed as descriptive propositions, or as address, or as speech-acts, without specifying which particular biblical genre we are considering. Of course, as Stanley Porter and Jason Robinson have re-

[1]Anthony C. Thiselton, *New Horizons in Hermeneutics* (London: HarperCollins; Grand Rapids: Zondervan, 1992). This, incidentally, has been republished in a new format in celebration of twenty years since its first publication, and Stephen Choi, one of my PhD graduates, has produced a Korean translation, which is a labor of love since it exceeds one thousand pages in Korean.

[2]Robert H. Gundry, *The Old Is Better: New Testament Essays in Support of Traditional Interpretation* (Tübingen: Mohr Siebeck, 2005), p. 399.

[3]Unless otherwise stated, Scripture quotations are taken from the New Revised Standard Version.

[4]George B. Caird, *The Revelation of St. John the Divine* (London: Black, 1996), p. 25 (my italics).

cently reminded us, books on exegesis rather than hermeneutics often do this, but as soon as writers engage with broader philosophical and theological problems they are seduced by a tendency to generalize.[5] Once again, Ludwig Wittgenstein offers a salutary warning against "our craving for generality," and "the contemptuous attitude towards the particular case."[6] Second, among those for whom it is important to stand in a Reformed theological tradition, there is much *mythology* and *misunderstanding* about the alleged Reformed commendation of one single simple meaning. This applies, for example, to John Calvin's comment that the exegete must grasp the true sense of Scripture that is genuine and simple (*qui germanus est et simplex*).[7]

As those irreproachably "Reformed" theologians G. C. Berkouwer and Herman Bavinck comment: "It is not until *post*-Reformation theology that a shift occurred: for the idea of perspicuity is then applied to the *words* of Scripture, particularly in their semantic function. In this manner Scripture is isolated from its context."[8] For the Reformers, especially Martin Luther and Calvin, they argue, *claritas* or perspicuity applied not to words and sentences, but to the message of salvation. The polemical context of their argument was the allegorical interpretation of doctrinal passages by the Roman Catholic Church, and Desiderius Erasmus's skepticism about whether the Bible gave clear enough messages for practical *action.*

Does this imply, then, that there are no constraints at all on pluralism in hermeneutics? Umberto Eco derives from Jurij Lotman the key contrast between *transmissive* texts, or "closed" texts, and *productive* texts, or "open" texts.[9] The simplest example of transmissive or "closed" texts

---

[5]Stanley E. Porter and Jason C. Robinson, *Hermeneutics: An Introduction to Interpretive Theory* (Grand Rapids: Eerdmans, 2011), pp. xvi-7 and throughout.

[6]Ludwig Wittgenstein, *The Blue and Brown Books* (Oxford: Blackwell, 1969), p. 18.

[7]John Calvin, *The Epistles of Paul to Galatians, Ephesians, Philippians and Colossians* (Edinburgh: Oliver & Boyd, 1965), p. 85.

[8]G. C. Berkouwer, *Studies in Dogmatics: Holy Scripture* (Grand Rapids: Eerdmans, 1975), p. 275 (my italics).

[9]Umberto Eco, *A Theory of Semiotics* (Bloomington, IN: Indiana University Press, 1976), pp. 136-39; cf. pp. 56, 135 and throughout; cf. Umberto Eco, *Semiotics and the Philosophy of Language* (London: MacMillan, 1984).

comes from engineering. A manual of instruction about how to mend a defect or failure in a given brand of car cannot and should not be interpreted pluralistically. The same principle would apply to a pharmacist's approach when following a doctor's medical prescription. The instructions should be followed closely step by step, as the manufacturer or doctor intends them to be followed. They presuppose certain *facts* that are given, whatever postmodernists may claim. It is notorious that in most universities the engineering faculty has little time for postmodernism. Yet, in the humanities, departments of language and literature often deal with literary, metaphorical, poetic or "open" texts, which have little or nothing to do with conveying information or facts. They often set the mind going in various directions. Lotman and Eco thus distinguish "handbook" texts from "productive" texts. In Paul Ricoeur's famous words, "Symbols give rise to thought."[10]

Clearly the biblical writings contain *both* types of texts. It may seem boring and "unliterary" simply to report facts, but the earliest Christian tradition reports the fact that Christ took a loaf of bread on the night when he was betrayed, and broke it (1 Cor 11:23-24); while the earliest Christian *kerygma* proclaims that "Christ died . . . that he was buried, [and] that he was raised on the third day" (1 Cor 15:3-4). With characteristic common sense, Graham Stanton long ago pointed out the foolishness of assuming that facts about Jesus, as Rudolf Bultmann had rashly claimed, held no interest for the followers of Jesus.[11] Even, however, such phrases as "he was raised" at once show the need for another level of interpretation. Eco has taken infinite trouble to illustrate criteria for the crucial difference between transmissive and literary texts, and Wittgenstein went to infinite trouble to show that stretches of language can simultaneously perform more than one function. Some may still recall Eco's example of the difference between the closed propo-

---

[10]Paul Ricoeur, *Freud and Philosophy: An Essay on Interpretations* (New Haven, CT, and London: Yale University Press, 1970), p. 543.

[11]Graham N. Stanton, *Jesus of Nazareth in New Testament Preaching* (Cambridge: Cambridge University Press, 1975), esp. pp. 137-71.

sition "Water-level ten feet," which conveys a fact, and the open statement "Water level dangerous," which conveys a value judgment.[12]

THE TWO TESTAMENTS: ALLEGORY, TYPOLOGY AND REREADING

The next reason for, or type of, plurality is more theologically motivated, and has a longer and more honorable history in the Bible, in the church fathers and in medieval exegesis. I confess that I have always found the issue ambivalent and at times a puzzle. During my years at Sheffield from 1970 onward, I found myself pulled in two opposite directions by colleagues. James Atkinson frequently quoted Luther and Augustine. Augustine declared, "Our Lord's cross was a key by which things that were closed were unlocked."[13] Similarly, everything in the Bible, Luther urged, serves to promote Christ. On the other hand, my Old Testament colleague David Clines observed that the problem with R. K. Harrison's commentary on Jeremiah was that every page implied that the book of Jeremiah would have been so much better a book if only it had been written by a Christian!

In an important sense, both were right. Hugh of St. Victor declared, "All of Divine Scripture is one book, and that one book is Christ, because all of Divine Scripture speaks of Christ . . . and is fulfilled in Christ."[14] Henri de Lubac exclaims that Jeremiah and the second part of Isaiah should be interpreted as "a new song," by rereading and meditating on the ancient texts in the light of later events or new situations, and a deeper understanding of theology.[15] But Henri de Lubac also stresses that the Old Testament must be allowed to speak *with its own voice*. After all, the Jews and the earliest Christians regarded the Torah and the Old Testament as Holy Scripture, revealed by God through the prophets. He

---

[12]Eco, *Theory of Semiotics*, p. 56; cf. pp. 135-39.
[13]Augustine, *On the Psalms*, Nicene and Post-Nicene Fathers series 2, vol. 8, p. 155.
[14]Hugh of St Victor, *On Noah's Ark* 2:8, Patrologia Latina vol. 176, col. 642c-d.
[15]Henri de Lubac, *Mediaeval Exegesis, vol. 1: The Four Senses of Scripture* (Grand Rapids: Eerdmans; Edinburgh: T & T Clark, 1998), p. 230.

also stresses the importance of the letter—history, or what he calls "the biblical facts."[16] He quotes the thirteenth-century aphorism: "The letter teaches us what was done."[17] If God reveals himself in and through the history of the world, we cannot ignore this historical meaning.

In fact the first clear formulation of Gregory the Great's fourfold meaning came from John Cassian, in his *First Conference* 14:8, namely that after historical interpretation, "spiritual" interpretation is of three kinds: tropological, allegorical and anagogical.[18] Cassian expounds how the letter teaches what God has done; the allegory teaches what we should believe; the moral what we should do; and the anagogical where we are heading. These represent the historical, theological, ethical and eschatological levels of meaning.

However, will viewing the text or meaning through the lens of knowledge of Christ and his work add a depth and fullness which derives both from recontextualizing it and rereading it from the vantage point of theology? The three traditional ways of describing this are *sensus plenior*, allegory and typology. Jerome comments, "We have drawn the lines of history: now let us set our hand to allegory."[19] Ambrose declares, "A higher sense calls us forth."[20] Augustine writes, "We have heard the facts; let us look into the mystery."[21] In the medieval period we could add Bede the Venerable, Hugh and many others.

It seems inescapable that we thus generate at least a twofold meaning. But we must be cautious on two grounds. First, the fathers often appeal to the precedent of Paul in Galatians. But Otto Michel and Leonhard Goppelt insist that Paul uses typology, not allegory, even though Paul's Greek word, *allēgoroumena*, seems to suggest allegory. Second, the dif-

---

[16]Henri de Lubac, *Mediaeval Exegesis, vol. 2, The Four Senses of Scripture* (Grand Rapids: Eerdmans; Edinburgh: T & T Clark, 2000), pp. 41-82.

[17]Ibid., p. 41.

[18]John Cassian, *First Conference* 14.8, Nicene and Post-Nicene Fathers series 2, vol. 11, p. 437.

[19]Jerome, *Letter* 52:10, Patrologia Latina vol. 25, col. 1063.

[20]Ambrose, *On Noah and the Ark* 11, Patrologia Latina vol. 14, col. 377c).

[21]Augustine, *Commentary on John* 50, Patrologia Latina vol. 35, col. 1760).

ficulty of finding and establishing *criteria* for the second meaning is notorious. It is admirably illustrated by the difference between Irenaeus and Clement of Alexandria. In Clement's work the so-called Christian gnostic finds secret "higher meanings" that may be perceived and preserved only by the elite "spirituals," transmitted in a secret tradition. In Irenaeus, by contrast, all meanings become part of a *public, assessable, testable tradition,* which all people are invited to compare with the apostles' teaching or the rule of faith. Allegory merely suggests a *parallelism between ideas;* typology rests on a *parallelism between events.* We could quote Richard Hanson, Geoffrey Lampe, Goppelt and many others to this effect.[22] In Gal 4:24-26 Paul has in mind a historical correspondence. Michel and Goppelt insist on regarding this as typology.[23] Earle Ellis and J. W. Aagerson prefer the broader term *correspondence.* Paul speaks explicitly of "type" in Rom 5:12-21 and 1 Cor 10:1-3.

I still find this, however, a puzzling question. Walter Moberly once took me to task in his very gracious way for my doing insufficient justice to the Old Testament. I cannot yet see beyond the need to distinguish between two interpretations—the immediate historical one and that which sees through the lens of the coming and the ministry of Christ. But I concede that Moberly, and now also Richard Briggs, have studied this issue more than I, and I defer to them and warmly commend their work.[24]

It is time to come more specifically to grips with what constitutes a *responsible* plurality in hermeneutics. In recent years I have been impressed by Hans Robert Jauss on reception theory and reception history, but more especially with Mikhail Bakhtin, who prefers the

---

[22]R. P. C. Hanson, *Allegory and Event* (London: SCM, 1959), p. 7; Geoffrey W. H. Lampe and Kenneth J. Woollcombe, *Essays on Typology* (London: SCM, 1957), p. 39.

[23]Otto Michel, *Paulus und seine Bible* (Guttersloh: Bertelsmann, 1929), p. 110; Leonhard Goppelt, *Typos: The Typological Interpretation of the Old Testament in the New* (Grand Rapids: Eerdmans, 1982), pp. 139-40.

[24]R. W. L. Moberly, *The Bible, Theology and Faith: A Study of Abraham and Jesus* (Cambridge: Cambridge University Press, 2000); idem, *The Theology of Genesis* (Cambridge: Cambridge University Press, 2009); and Richard S. Briggs and Joel N. Lohr, *A Theological Introduction to the Pentateuch* (Grand Rapids: Baker Academic, 2012), and some twenty-nine of Walter Moberly's research articles cited therein.

term *polyphonic meaning* to *pluralism*. Bakhtin welcomes what some may call pluralism, but he emphatically rejects relativism and prefers the term *concordance* to *unity*. Concordance is his preferred term for what the "biblical theology" movement would call *unity*. I will come to Bakhtin shortly.

PLURALISM, FORMATION AND POLYPHONIC MEANING

There must be limits to pluralistic interpretation in many parts, but *not every* part, of the Bible. In *Hermeneutics of Doctrine*[25] I expanded on *formation* as the aim of encounter with the Bible. Frances Young and David Kelsey had talked about the role of the Bible in *shaping* readers' identities, and the subtitle of *New Horizons* used the word *transforming* in this sense. I cited some Anglican theologians, such as Philip Turner, and even secular philosophers, such as Hans-Georg Gadamer and Jauss, in urging this function. Formation reorientates disposition and character.

Yet if *every* text can be interpreted in an endlessly pluralistic way, how can this "form" or "transform" readers *in a specific direction*? In my Chester Inaugural Lecture *Can the Bible Mean Whatever We Want It to Mean?* I took the example of Laban's words in Gen 31:49, "The Lord watch between you and me, when we are absent one from the other." Numerous Christians have used this text as a fond commitment of a loved one to God as they part for a period. It seems to commend the two to God's protection. But the context *excludes* this meaning. From Genesis 29 onward, Jacob and Laban play one dastardly trick after another on each other, culminating in Jacob's thinking he had married Rachel, but when he awoke in the morning, the Hebrew dramatically reads: *ba-bōker wĕhinēh-hû' lē'āh*: "In the morning—look!—Leah!" (Gen 29:25). So when they part, did they commit each other to God's loving protection or care? Laban declares: "May the Lord glue his eyes on you, and *avenge* me if you try one more dastardly trick!"

Probably the greatest skepticism about biblical truth today arises

---

[25]Anthony C. Thiselton, *The Hermeneutics of Doctrine* (Grand Rapids and Cambridge: Eerdmans, 2007).

from the mistaken notion that you can make the Bible mean anything you like. We must resist this by applying questions about context, genre and formation. We must be cautious about pluralism, especially in *historical report* or in *theology*. I will develop these issues further later. Meanwhile, do all "literary" texts allow for pluralism? Roland Barthes's *Mythologies* shows the limitations of what some call the "natural" meaning, even in everyday texts. For example, he claims that such pictures as that of a black soldier saluting the French flag may not so much "describe" an event as convey an imperialist message.[26] Describing a furniture arrangement or the choice of particular clothes or even beards may convey a message about class or social attitudes. These may suggest how we wish to be perceived. But this is not the main kind of pluralism with which we are concerned. Not only Barthes but also Wittgenstein shows that, without a constraining *context*, in his words, "A picture, whatever it may be, can be variously interpreted."[27] (This makes me anxious about some of the medieval mystics and much supposed "prophecy" in the popular sense today. The meaning of "pictures" is far from self-evident.) Wittgenstein cites the example of a picture representing a boxer in a particular stance and comments: "This picture can be used to tell someone how he should stand . . . or how he should *not* hold himself; or how a man did stand in such-and-such a place."[28] Only the context (and perhaps an agreed training) will limit a pluralism against unmeant or irrelevant possibilities.

BAKHTIN ON POLYPHONIC MEANING

I come now to Bakhtin. Much more relevant to biblical interpretation is Mikhail Bakhtin's distinctive notion of *polyphonic voices*, which he ascribes to Fyodor Dostoevsky. Bakhtin is the theorist; Dostoevsky is the practitioner. Bakhtin (1895–1975) defines polyphony as "a plurality of independent and unmerged voices and consciousnesses," and comments,

---

[26]Roland Barthes, *Mythologies* (London: Jonathan Cape, 1972), pp. 15-25, 91-93, 116-20.
[27]Ludwig Wittgenstein, *Zettel* (Oxford: Blackwell, 1967), sect. 236.
[28]Wittgenstein, *Philosophical Investigations* (Oxford: Blackwell, 1958), p. 11.

*A genuine polyphony of fully valid voices is in fact the chief character-
istic of Dostoevsky's novels.* What unfolds in his work is not just a
multitude of characters . . . in a single objective world . . . ; rather
a plurality of consciousnesses *with equal rights* and *each with its
own world.*[29]

Kevin Vanhoozer is right to compare Bakhtin's polyphony with the
voices of the biblical canon, as I have in *Hermeneutics of Doctrine*. But I
doubt whether Vanhoozer's analogies and parallels really grasp the distinctiveness and subtlety of Bakhtin or Dostoevsky.[30] (1) Bakhtin
stresses that the "voices" come from a plurality of *subjects,* not objects,
or passive object-like things; (2) the "unity," or, better, the "concordance"
between the voices is of "a *higher order*" than mere coherence or unity,
like the "complex" world of Albert Einstein rather than that of Sir Isaac
Newton; (3) the multiple voices do *not* imply a kind of *relativism*; (4)
each voice speaks *from within its own distinctive world*, not from a
common world; (5) the dialogue occurs between *equally valued* voices,
and *never* reaches "*finality*"; and (6) each voice speaks and addresses the
reader directly, rather than as a *secondhand construct.*[31] The voices are not
described; "they describe themselves . . . never represented secondhand."[32] Two of the greatest experts on this subject, Gary Morson and
Bakhtin's translator and editor Caryl Emerson, fully endorse this distinctive description of Bakhtin's polyphony and "Prosaics."[33] They also
stress the *creativity* of Bakhtin's Dostoevsky and the place he gives to
surprise and novelty. This is one reason why the dialogue of voices has
no predetermined end. They write: "Polyphony was essentially a theory

---

[29]Mikhail Bakhtin, *Problems of Dostoevsky's Poetics* (Minneapolis and London: University of
Minnesota Press, 1984), p. 6 (his italics first, then mine).

[30]Kevin Vanhoozer, *The Drama of Doctrine: A Canonical-Linguistic Approach to Christian
Theology* (Louisville: Westminster John Knox, 2005), pp. 272-75; Thiselton, *Hermeneutics
of Doctrine*, pp. 134-44.

[31]Bakhtin, *Problems of Dostoevsky's Poetics*, pp. 7, 16, 48, 69, 93, 105, 166, 272 and 289.

[32]Ibid., p. 48.

[33]Gary Saul Morson and Caryl Emerson, *Mikhail Bakhtin: Creation of a Prosaics* (Stanford,
CA: Stanford University Press, 1990), pp. 231-34, 237-40, 243-68.

of creativity. . . . The polyphonic author . . . makes surprise part of his design."[34] This is one important reason why it becomes hazardous to speak with any confidence about the future of biblical interpretation.

DIFFERENT LEVELS OF POLYPHONIC OR PLURALIST MEANING: FROM CANON TO POSTMODERNISM

From the Scripture and Hermeneutics series,[35] one of the most important volumes, I think, is the seventh, namely *Canon and Biblical Interpretation*. I wrote an introduction to volume 7, with a concluding section on "Polyphonic Voices, Canon, and Theological Construction."[36] I and fellow contributors noted, for example, that the problem of suffering in the Bible could be addressed only by putting the *more optimistic voices* of Deuteronomy and Proverbs alongside the more *pessimistic or realistic voices* of Job, Ecclesiastes, Psalms of lament, and perhaps Lamentations. Gordon McConville, Gordon Wenham, Tremper Longman and Robin Parry amplified this approach. Similarly the optimism of Joshua and the realism of Judges represent the different voices that, as in Bakhtin's polyphonic voices, speak as subjects from their own world. They speak a different but complementary message. As Bakhtin on Dostoevsky stresses, the interaction between these voices can never be finalized, or they then cease to be creative. *To call these "contradictions," as Heikki Räisänen does, is to miss the point, and has nothing in common with polyphony in Bakhtin.*[37] *This could not be a "contradiction" since the conversation continues without finality. It constitutes an ongoing process within the canon,* in which several voices speak as *subjects* from their own context and world. Again, Bakhtin likens their unity to that of an Einsteinian

---

Morson and Emerson, *Mikhail Bakhtin*, p. 257; cf. Karina Clark and Michael Holquist, *Mikhail Bakhtin* (Cambridge, MA: Harvard University Press, 1984), pp. 238-52.

[35]Series eds. Craig Bartholomew and Anthony Thiselton (Grand Rapids: Zondervan, 2000–2007), 8 volumes.

[36]Craig Bartholomew et al., eds., *Canon and Biblical Interpretation* (Grand Rapids: Zondervan, 2006), pp. 24-27.

[37]Heikki Räisänen, *Challenges to Biblical Interpretation: Collected Essays 1991-2000* (London and Boston: Brill, 2001), p. 229.

universe, in which no single voice drowns out the other.

We encounter an insoluble problem, however, in Jean-François Lyotard, especially in his postmodern notion of *The Differend*.[38] In his view, genuine dialogue is a masquerade. Here we encounter a different kind of plurality, if it really is one. Whichever is the stronger voice within a dialogue drowns out the weaker, by determining the rules and definitions of the game, or what might count as a criterion in adversarial dialogue. Thus Lyotard is one of the most damaging enemies of hermeneutics. Whereas Bakhtin explicitly rejects the concept of "incommensurability," a term drawn from the philosophy of science, Lyotard appeals to it. He argues that there is no way of adjudicating between two irreconcilable points of view. In his book *Just Gaming*, he defends pluriformity.[39] Each point of view, he argues, depends on a different world of stories and narratives. He holds a radical pluralism at least as strong as that of Friedrich Nietzsche or Richard Rorty. He explicitly calls his pluralistic view *paganism*, in contrast to the more unified view of monotheism. Yet although this pluralism appears liberating, he argues in *The Differend*, a plurality of views becomes a device to disempower the weak and to dismiss the rational or truthful as sheer illusion. Rationality is always defined in the terms laid down by the strong, the predominant or the oppressor. Lyotard writes: "I would like to call a *differend* the case where a plaintiff is divested of all the means to argue, and becomes for that reason a victim."[40] Allegedly, because there are no metanarratives, we cannot even establish, he claims, whether, for example, there ever was in history an empirical Auschwitz. Lyotard barely recognizes *any* notion of *responsibility*. He claims, "Obligation cannot be justified."[41]

We have just compared two different levels of pluralistic or poly-

---

[38]Jean-François Lyotard, *The Differend: Phrases in Dispute* (Manchester, UK: Manchester University Press, 1990).

[39]Jean-François Lyotard, *Just Gaming* (Manchester, UK: Manchester University Press, 1985).

[40]Lyotard, *The Differend*, p. 9.

[41]Lyotard, *Just Gaming*, p. 22.

phonic readings of texts. The first provides a *legitimate* and *responsible* plurality by placing alongside one another different traditions within the biblical canon, and grouped with this is polyphonic dialogue in Bakhtin. Because these traditions do *not* represent final *"contradictions,"* this does not exclude systematic theology, provided that this recognizes, with Bakhtin, the right of each theological voice to speak out its own world and context and not to become assimilated to the other. I agree with Bakhtin that to speak of *concordance* here may be more accurate than to speak of unity, as if the dialogue had *reached finality.* The second approach constitutes a very different notion of plurality. Lyotard, in contrast to Bakhtin, insists that one voice, in the end, must appropriate, assimilate and overcome the voice of the other. Although Lyotard may appear to write as a postmodernist, and to approve of fragmentation and pluralism, ultimately he evaporates it of any meaning. He does *not* advocate a *responsible* plurality. He offers a disguised *totalitarianism.* Hermeneutics becomes impossible, for the *patience, tolerance and respect for the other, which Emilio Betti sees as the heart of hermeneutics, have been excluded.* Hermeneutics returns to becoming an instrumental tool, against which long ago Friedrich Schleiermacher protested.

Somewhere in between these two opposite ways of understanding pluriform or polyphonic reading stands a third approach, namely that of Hans Robert Jauss. Certainly he stands nearer to intracanonical readings and to Bakhtin than to Lyotard. Jauss speaks explicitly of three levels or horizons of reading.[42] The first level or horizon is virtually *prereflective and perceptive,* and would probably be akin to a preliminary understanding, preunderstanding or intuitive understanding. The second approximates to traditional modern exegesis. The third is primarily applicatory. It asks, what does this text say to me in my situation? Clearly in Jauss this largely depends on two factors. First a horizon of *expectations:* what do I expect the text to say in view of previous readings and of my own situation? This is helpful and positive for hermeneutics.

---

[42]Hans Robert Jauss, *Toward an Aesthetic of Reception* (Minneapolis: University of Minnesota Press, 1982), pp. 139-85.

Second, in reception history the changing context and historicality, or the historical situatedness of the reader or his or her reading community, plays a decisive part in generating meaning. This is also helpful.

This third level of plurality is more widespread and less surprising that it might seem. Even Wolfhart Pannenberg writes: "In a changed situation the traditional phrases, even when recited literally, do not mean what they did at the time of their original formulation."[43] Gerhard Ebeling makes exactly the same point; Pannenberg calls this "the hermeneutical problem."[44] Jauss's own solution, however, is to inquire into both the *continuities and discontinuities* of reception history. He looks for a *stable core of meaning* in how different communities of readers receive a text. Is such and such a reading maverick or eccentric? Or does it reflect a stable core of continuity? Sometimes, however, a novel reading may seem bold and creative. Here *horizon* becomes a better term than *level*, for it denotes the point of view that is at first constrained by the reader's circumstance in history, but is also capable of movement and expansion.

The major problem with reception history is that it tends to give an equal acceptance to various interpretations that reflect given horizons. This is why I retain a certain caution about it, alongside approval. This caution is more marked in the case of some kinds of liberation theology, postcolonial hermeneutics and some kinds of feminist theology. These often become overselective in what they see as the use or "point" of certain biblical passages.

THE FUTURE OF BIBLICAL INTERPRETATION

As I commented at the beginning of this chapter, to predetermine where we are going stifles the *creativity*. We cannot change our minds or change the direction in which we are traveling. This point has been well expounded by Bakhtin. However, we are entitled to consider *not future directions, but future possibilities.*

(1) I want to hold together two arguments. First, Stanley Porter

---

[43]Wolfhart Pannenberg, *Basic Questions in Theology* (London: SCM, 1970), 1:9.
[44]Ibid., pp. 10-11.

stresses the distinction between genuine hermeneutics, which involve biblical, theological, philosophical and linguistic issues, and mere handbooks of biblical exegesis. Second, I am aware of Walter Moberly's (and others') concern that hermeneutics should not merely generalize but be rooted in specific biblical texts. I have always aimed at this, but may at times not have done this enough. The nearest positive example is *New Horizons in Hermeneutics*, and in terms of doctrine, in *The Hermeneutics of Doctrine*. The next generation of books on hermeneutics will need to draw broadly on a variety of interdisciplinary fields, but also constantly illustrate its work with reference to *specific* biblical texts.

(2) Second, it may be encouraging to reflect what hermeneutics might *not* be. It is encouraging to see, for example, that the brief excursion of *Semeia* and other works into structuralism and poststructuralism seems to have drained the subject almost dry. I also wonder how seriously postcolonial and liberation hermeneutics will still run, given that they almost always use the same familiar texts for their own purposes. Reader-response theory may deserve a little more mileage as a way of ensuring that the *reader engages actively and not passively* with the text. But I am still doubtful whether a sufficient number of biblical scholars see that the Bible concerns engagement with the Other, and does not constitute primarily a mirror in which the wishes and desires of the self are bounced back, clothed with pseudo-divine authority.

(3) My readers will know that I have often drawn on particular thinkers, sometimes Christian and sometimes secular, as starting-points for further ideas. In this essay I have drawn a little on Hans Robert Jauss, and more on Mikhail Bakhtin. There may still be mileage in reception history, as Ulrich Luz indicates. There is probably more to be learned from Bakhtin's notion of polyphonic voices as he sees them in Dostoevsky. Bakhtin insists not only that each voice must be given equal weight, but that they must speak from within their world. This seems to me to be true of the biblical canon, and of the four Gospels. On this particular issue, systematic theology should be cautious. Here the word *synthesis* is not helpful.

(4) We cannot surrender to the kind of dissolution of hermeneutics that Lyotard's *The Differend* or *Just Gaming* would imply. *Rationality* is one of the most precious gifts that God has given us. To try to submerge or describe it by borrowing from the philosophy of science the term *incommensurability* is an insult to what has been given to humankind. I am astonished that so many devout Christians look toward post-modernism merely because it attacks the hegemony of scientific knowledge and the Enlightenment. Either wholesale approval or wholesale rejection of postmodernism seems to me misguided and naive. But if hermeneutics is to survive, its worst excesses must be resisted.

(5) There remains a vast set of issues concerning which I am simply unsure of the future but harbor the hope of further advances. Have we yet harvested all that can be gathered from *speech-act theory*? In 1992, when I wrote *New Horizons*, I argued that we had found in speech-act theory a breakthrough in Christology. The effectiveness of the speech-acts of Jesus depended on his identity.[45] But many readers seemed to lose sight of the role of *presupposition and convention or, in theology, of covenant*. Richard Briggs's book, *Words in Action*, promotes a valiant attempt at exploration.[46] Much literature on this subject, however, is admittedly sometimes disappointing.

(6) *Literary theory* has been responsible for some of the worst blind alleys in biblical scholarship. I still recall a Cambridge biblical professor rehearsing the so-called genetic fallacy as if it were undisputed truth, without realizing that its originators applied it only to poetry and symbol. Indeed if we are looking at Job or Jonah I am not certain that it is wholly wrong. But it was George Caird in the 1960s and 1970s who encouraged me to throw the net wide in New Testament research. He suggested that New Testament studies had reached an impasse, because the same old assumptions and aphorisms were incestuously shared among New Testament scholars alone. Perhaps, if we extend our net, we

---

45Thiselton, *New Horizons in Hermeneutics*, pp. 272-79, 283-312.
46Richard S. Briggs, *Words in Action: Speech-Act Theory and Biblical Interpretation* (Edinburgh: T & T Clark, 2001).

may be able to do better. For example, we did well to draw on such works as those of Gérard Genette and Robert Alter. Genette explored the concept of *narrative time*, in contrast to chronological time.[47] On this basis he gives us an important key to reading Mark. Mark initially begins at a fast pace; slows down in the middle chapters; and then portrays the passion and events of the cross in slow motion. The cross, he says, is what the whole Gospel is leading toward. Narrative time transforms questions of chronological discrepancy into irrelevance. To ask about chronological discrepancies or harmonies between the Gospels often appears naive in the light of narrative time and the diverse uses of time among authors. Further, Alter rejected the notion of a doublet of contradictory sources behind the call of David in 1–2 Samuel. Like Bakhtin, he proposed two *complementary* points of view, each of which addresses its own world. The short episode of the anointing of David represented the point of view of divine decree (1 Sam 16:12-13); the long episode involving Goliath and Saul represented the viewpoint of the "brawling chaos of everyday life" (1 Sam 17–2 Sam 5:5).[48]

Who knows, certainly not I, where the explorer will next strike gold? But this is the essence of genuine research!

---

[47]Gérard Genette, *Narrative Discourse* (Ithaca, NY: Cornell University Press, 1981), chaps. 4-6.
[48]Robert Alter, *The Art of Biblical Narrative* (New York: Basic Books, 1981), pp. 147-53.

atics and interpretation
mous or even inclusive
icated upon—whether
, but biblical interpre-
elements. Biblical inter-
sults of how the Bible is
odern allegorizing, liter-
xegesis, textual or lower
ch as form, source and
ontemporary methods
eological criticisms and
less influenced by these
cal interpretation is her-
if many interpreters are
mply "reading the text."
outside the scope of in-
retation—including the
even its methods—that
pt that such acts inevi-

eutics? The formulation
ubcategory of the wider
he Bible. In other words,
ith the Bible as its object
cs, however, is in ways a
utics from its inception
anding the Bible. From
e conditions for under-
al tradition has been a
one of the major herme-
a contemporary person

: An Introduction to Interpretive

2

Biblical Hermeneutics
and *Theological* Responsibility

Stanley E. Porter

INTRODUCTION

I am honored to contribute to this important and illustrious project, arising from a conference held in honor of my former doctoral supervisor, Professor Anthony Thiselton, and with the intention of advancing the agenda that he has so ably and almost singlehandedly established in the areas of biblical interpretation and hermeneutics. The tripartite distinction in the formulation of the title of the book in many ways encapsulates the work of Professor Thiselton. Professor Thiselton has always been a biblical interpreter. His massive commentary on 1 Corinthians is more than sufficient evidence to establish this point, but it can be supplemented by numerous other works, such as his work on biblical words and their supposed power, biblical semantics, and the Thessalonian letters.[1] Professor Thiselton is also identified with responsible plurality in his bib-

---

[1]For Professor Thiselton's bibliography, see Stanley E. Porter and Matthew R. Malcolm, "The Life and Work of Anthony Charles Thiselton," in *Horizons in Hermeneutics: A Festschrift in Honor of Anthony C. Thiselton*, ed. Stanley E. Porter and Matthew R. Malcolm (Grand Rapids: Eerdmans, 2013).

lical interpretation. This is evidenced from start to
arship—from exploration of such scholars as Martin
Bultmann, Hans-Georg Gadamer and Ludwig Wittg
major monograph, to presenting a panoply of contemp
in his major constructive work, to his exploration of d
great monograph. Plurality is in abundant evidence (the
clearly drawn, for example at such practices as neoprag
reading), but it is always responsible plurality, the type
affirming various theological doctrines. Professor Thi
identified with biblical hermeneutics. Despite the recent
in so-called theological interpretation (which Professor
highly influenced, whether intentionally or not), I do n
there is any contemporary biblical scholar who has done n
introduce and explain biblical hermeneutics to his conter
others in biblical studies than has Professor Thiselton—t
becoming identified with the subject in many spheres. He
fundamental and deep work of ploughing through the majc
the last one hundred or more years (indeed, even back
Schleiermacher and others) and finding common thoughts
to tie them together in a contemporary exposition and even
He does not shy away from the hard work of interpretation i
servience to the larger hermeneutical task, refusing to take the
dirty or glib and witty means of addressing an issue.

It is within this light that I wish to address the topic of m
There is no way that this chapter can constitute an exposition
neutics, or even of biblical hermeneutics. It is instead a treatm
interface of biblical hermeneutics and theological responsibili
I believe that these are topics close to the front of Professor Th
professional and, I do not hesitate to say, personal interests, as a
who is concerned that the academic work that he does has a mea
relationship with his personal Christian beliefs and who he is as a
Yet, as Professor Thiselton has also evidenced within his works—
not say often, but at crucial points at the least—definitions o

---

Gadamer has so ably shown). Instead, hermene
are intersecting and overlapping but not synony
terms. Biblical interpretation no doubt is pre
knowingly or unknowingly—a hermeneutics
tation also involves other practical and applied
pretation includes the theories, methods and re
interpreted, whether this involves ancient or m
alism, harmonization, grammatical-historical e
criticism, various so-called higher criticisms su
redaction criticism, and so-called modern or
such as literary readings, canonical readings, id
the like, which result in readings of texts more or
and other methods. There is no doubt that bibl
meneutically motivated and responsive—even
not cognizant of this and believe they are si
There is much involved in hermeneutics that is
terpretation, just as there are elements of interp
mechanics or techniques of interpretation, and
are outside the purview of hermeneutics, exc
tably reflect prior hermeneutical commitments

Where then does that leave biblical hermen
seems to imply that biblical hermeneutics is a s
field of hermeneutics, but concentrating upon t
it is a type of so-called general hermeneutics, w
of interpretive theorizing. Biblical hermeneuti
terminological redundancy, because hermene
has been associated with theology and unders
Schleiermacher to the present, examining th
standing the Christian theological and textu
major focus of hermeneutics.[3] This is because
neutical challenges is posed by the Bible—how

[3]See Stanley E. Porter and Jason C. Robinson, *Hermeneutics*
Theory (Grand Rapids: Eerdmans, 2011), pp. 24-33.

understands an ancient document, with all that that implies regarding the historical-cultural situatedness of both the ancient text and modern reader. More than that, there is the challenge of how a contemporary person reads such a document in the light of a developing history of its understanding by other interpreters in their varied lives, places and circumstances. For many of us, the hermeneutical challenge also includes how to appropriate such understanding of a document that is accepted by the church as canonical, believed to have been divinely inspired, and accepted as authoritative for Christian life and practice. These are not small demands. Hidden within them, however, are the major challenges that hermeneutics has continued to wrestle with. Many different metaphors have been devised to address some of these hermeneutical challenges, such as circles, spirals, horizons and triads—each one of them capturing something of the challenge of bridging the subject-object divide, and each one of them failing to capture what is most crucial, the complexity of the hermeneutical task.

Is biblical hermeneutics then simply hermeneutics, but of the Bible? In one sense, that is probably an accurate assessment. However, there is something apparently inadequate in simply talking about biblical hermeneutics without talking about the Bible itself and attempting to understand it. In a recent volume that I coedited with Beth Stovell, entitled *Biblical Hermeneutics: Five Views*, we faced a similar issue. In devising the scope of this book, we were compelled to narrow the subject of hermeneutics to ways that biblical hermeneutics is actually formulated. As a result, we have contributions in five areas: historical-critical/grammatical, literary/postmodern, redemptive-historical, canonical and philosophical/theological. Each hermeneutical stance was grounded differently: whether in the intention of the author as discerned through historical-grammatical means, the text as literary document, redemption history, the canonical community, and reception- and presupposition-circumscribed plurality. As a result, all but philosophical/theological hermeneutics offered readings of a chosen passage in order to demonstrate the interpretive results of their biblical-hermeneutical method. In that sense, such readings went beyond the scope of hermeneutics more narrowly defined and crossed over to biblical interpretation. The philosophical/theological hermeneut explicitly declined such an attempt, in Gadamerian and Ricoeurian fashion not wanting to equate hermeneutics with either authorial meaning or method.[4] We could debate whether the philosophical/theological hermeneut could have at least given some indications of where such a hermeneutical stance could have led, or whether another hermeneut would have done differently. The point, however, is that, in a book such as this, we could probably only reasonably expect one of the five hermeneutical positions not to offer a reading of the text—because for biblical hermeneutics the Bible is integral to the hermeneutical enterprise, especially the forms of biblical hermeneutics represented. In fact, not only was hermeneutics born out of discussion of Christian theology and the Bible, but since that time, even though hermeneutics as a discipline has continued to develop apart from biblical understanding, there are distinctive hermeneutical stances toward the Bible that have been developed to address the questions of the Bible. In particular, among the five noted above, one might well identify the redemptive-historical and canonical approaches in this way, as well as the particular form of historical-critical/grammatical hermeneutics as outlined by the particular contributor to the volume. In other words, when we speak of hermeneutics, we need not speak of the Bible. But when we speak of biblical hermeneutics, we often speak of a particular kind of biblical hermeneutics. In this sense, biblical hermeneutics often crosses the divide from general to special hermeneutics, that is, it becomes a type of hermeneutics—whether for good or bad—that is only applied to the Bible.

This complex of issues raises a set of questions that are not easily resolved—and certainly will not be resolved by me here. They involve all of the fundamental questions related to hermeneutics and under-

---

[4]See Stanley E. Porter and Beth M. Stovell, eds., *Biblical Hermeneutics: Five Views* (Downers Grove, IL: IVP Academic, 2012), with contributions by Craig L. Blomberg, F. Scott Spencer, Richard B. Gaffin Jr., Robert W. Wall and Merold Westphal.

standing. They include at least the following: what is the basis of understanding in a biblical hermeneutics? Is biblical hermeneutics foundationalist (even objectivist), grounded in the author of Scripture (whether human or divine); antifoundationalist, with no objectivist basis; or postfoundationalist, recognizing the infinite complexity of human situatedness and the attempt to make meaning of our surroundings? What role do such things as prior commitments, presuppositions, tradition, authority, the Bible and theology play in a biblical hermeneutics? What is the role of the self in understanding, and what is the role of the community? How do we differentiate among author, text and reader, and such things as authorial and textual intention? What are the relations between the individual elements of a text and the whole of a text? What role does textual and interpretive situatedness play? What role does the history of interpretation play? What are the differences among such terms as meaning, interpretation, significance and criticism, among others? All attempts at hermeneutics must come to terms with these factors in some way or another—whether the emphasis is upon authorial intention, the meaning of the text or the role of the reader, to identify the three main foci.

The complexity of these issues is made more difficult by the failure to differentiate two important questions that need to be differentiated: what did the text mean when it was composed by its author for its original audience, and what does the text mean for us today as modern readers? There have been many different answers to this question, with hermeneuts emphasizing one or the other question and tending to emphasize either ancient meaning or modern understanding. The classic distinction is E. D. Hirsch's between meaning and significance, with meaning what was intended by the author and significance what this meaning means in other contexts.[5] Many have rejected such a formulation as failing to realize that, apart from the author, the text transcends

---

[5]E. D. Hirsch Jr., *Validity in Interpretation* (New Haven, CT: Yale University Press, 1967), p. 8. See also P. D. Juhl, *Interpretation: An Essay in the Philosophy of Literary Criticism* (Princeton, NJ: Princeton University Press, 1980).

its original context and speaks in new ways to new audiences. Gadamer, Jacques Derrida, Roland Barthes, Paul Ricoeur, Michel Foucault and Paul de Man, among others—an intriguing group to be sure—all seem to argue similarly that the author has a fundamental role even if superseded in some way.[6] Wendell Harris takes a mediating position, in which interpretation is the probable meaning in the assumed authorial audience, while significance is related to nonauthorial contexts.[7] Gadamer differentiates between reproductive and productive meaning, Barthes speaks of giving the text autonomy free from the author, Derrida says that "doubling commentary," or reproducing the original meaning of a text, has a place in critical understanding, Ricoeur recognizes authorial intention but speaks of the text not coinciding with it once it is autonomous but needing to be "recontextualized," Foucault acknowledges the embeddedness of the author in the text, and de Man recognizes the place of grammar and its meaning even if he wishes to offset it with rhetoric. In other words, the question for hermeneutics is not what the text meant—which apparently hermeneuts and interpreters on all sides of the question can agree that it did at one time, even if this is difficulty conceived—but what does the text mean, today and in our situatedness as contemporary interpreters. Even if there is still disagreement on the first part of this formulation, the second appears to be the major hermeneutical question, biblical or otherwise. I am so bold

---

[6]Hans Georg Gadamer, *Truth and Method*, 2nd ed., trans. Joel Weinsheimer and Donald Marshall (New York: Crossroad, 1989), pp. 296-97; Roland Barthes, "The Death of the Author," in his *The Rustle of Language*, trans. Richard Howard (New York: Hill and Wang, 1986), pp. 49-55; Jacques Derrida, *On Grammatology*, trans. Gayatri Chakravorty Spivak (Baltimore, MD: Johns Hopkins University Press, 1976), p. 158; Paul Ricoeur, *Hermeneutics and the Human Sciences*, trans. John B. Thompson (New York: Cambridge University Press, 1981), pp. 91, 108, 139, 203; Michel Foucault, "What Is an Author?" in *The Foucault Reader*, ed. Paul Rabinow (New York: Pantheon, 1984), pp. 101-20 (111-12); and Paul de Man, "Semiology and Rhetoric," in *The Critical Tradition: Classic Texts and Contemporary Trends*, 2nd ed., ed. David H. Richter (Boston: Bedford, 1998), pp. 906-16 (908-9). I am thankful for the essay by Merold Westphal, "The Philosophical/Theological View," in *Biblical Hermeneutics*, pp. 70-88 (76-81), for some of the references here, although he would probably disagree with my use of them. For a fuller version of his treatment, see Westphal, *Whose Community? Which Interpretation?* (Grand Rapids: Baker, 2009), pp. 35-68.

[7]Wendell V. Harris, *Interpretive Acts in Search of Meaning* (Oxford: Clarendon, 1988), p. ix.

as to think that a robust hermeneutic can be developed that addresses both questions adequately, when interpretation is considered as consisting along two axes—one a synchronic one with clausal semantics and discourse semantics at opposite ends, and the other a diachronic one with the ancient context and the contemporary context at its poles—in light of which the various issues raised above find their appropriate place of address. However, this is not the place to explicate such an approach to hermeneutical understanding.

In this section, I have attempted to define hermeneutics in a way that sets the stage for discussion of theological responsibility. What I think is important to grasp is that the dispute over meaning in texts is not over whether texts can be interpreted, but whether interpretation is confined to the original ancient context or must be recontextualized or semantically productive in the context of the contemporary reader to have fulfilled the hermeneutical mandate. Hermeneutic theory indicates that a text is not adequately understood until it is understood in the present. Or, as Westphal says of the question for biblical hermeneutics, "What *is* God *saying* to us here and now through these words of Scripture?"[8]

WHAT IS THEOLOGICAL RESPONSIBILITY WITHIN A HERMENEUTICAL CONTEXT?

What, then, is theological responsibility within a hermeneutical context? There has been much made recently of the work of theological interpretation to mediate the gap between general or special hermeneutics and the Christian theological tradition. Before we simply accept that theological interpretation has met the burden of theological responsibility in biblical hermeneutics, I think that some comments are in order. At the outset, I think that a fundamental distinction must be made between theological hermeneutics and theological interpretation. These are often confused, to the detriment of theological hermeneutics and the misrepresentation of theological interpretation. However, by ex-

---

[8]Westphal, "Philosophical/Theological View," p. 79.

ploring the nature of theological interpretation, I believe that we can gain insight into a responsible theological hermeneutics.

Theological hermeneutics, in many ways pioneered by Professor Thiselton, is the attempt "to find an appropriate hermeneutic that is faithful to the Christian theological tradition,"[9] that is, demonstrate theological responsibility. Thus, in distinction from (simply) hermeneutics or even biblical hermeneutics, theological hermeneutics is a fairly recent development within the last part of the twentieth century as a conscious and explicit effort to bring hermeneutics and Christian theology into a mutually instructive dialogue—although to be sure there have been predecessors interested in the relationship of Christian theology and philosophy, even hermeneutics, before this time. Theological hermeneutics as I am defining it here is a recent phenomenon that has arisen in the aftermath of serious interest in hermeneutics in theological studies, and is distinguished by a number of characteristics. These include at least the following: bringing to bear the weight of philosophical thought on biblical interpretation, especially as that has been found in the Continental tradition, including but not exclusively focusing upon phenomenology (especially Gadamer and Ricoeur); a philosophically grounded attempt to establish at least the conditions for determinative meanings, even in the light of subsequent modern and postmodern thought; attention to those philosophers who have preserved or reinvigorated the Cartesian subject-object relationship, while avoiding the dangers of objectivism on the one hand and subjectivism and relativity on the other; an appreciation of the historic doctrines of the Christian church; an attention to ordinary language philosophy with its interest in functional language, especially as found in speech-act theory (or philosophy, as it is sometimes labeled), as a means of attempting to capture the power of the biblical witness and theological doctrines in the lives of its hearers/readers; and incorporation of reception history into hermeneutical thought, following the work of Ga-

---

[9]Porter and Robinson, *Hermeneutics*, p. 245.

damer and Jauss. I realize that this description is particularly amenable to a characerization of some of the major work of Professor Thiselton, but I think that many of the tenets would also describe others who would fall within the category of practicing theological hermeneutics.[10] Theological interpretation, however, as I have already indicated, needs to be distinguished from theological hermeneutics. They have a common origin, I believe, in the influence of several major theological hermeneuts. As noted above, theological hermeneutics in a sense goes back earlier to those with concerns for interpreting the Bible in the light of the church's theological affirmations. In that sense, both theological hermeneutics and theological interpretation share a common concern for finding a theologically and biblically grounded theological understanding of the Christian tradition that is virbrant and responsive to contemporary Christian thought and practice, rather than being at odds with a sterile tradition that is seen to have been created by historical criticism. However, unlike theological hermeneutics, theological interpretation has caused a groundswell of recent interest, such that there are numerous volumes both summarizing theological interpretation and exemplifying it in practice. The result has been the advocacy of a number of different forms of theological interpretation and an even larger number of theological interpretations of the Bible. In a recent paper, I distilled the major tenets of theological interpretation on the basis of five recent summative treatments.[11] There are six tenets. The first is, as

---

[10]Others who would fit to varying degrees would include Kevin Vanhoozer (see Porter and Robinson, *Hermeneutics*, pp. 258-66), Jens Zimmermann (*Recovering Theological Hermeneutics: An Incarnational-Trinitarian Theory of Interpretation* [Grand Rapids: Baker, 2004]), and Westphal ("Philosophical/Theological View").

[11]Stanley E. Porter, "What Exactly Is Theological Interpretation of Scripture, and Is It Hermeneutically Robust Enough for the Task to Which It Has Been Appointed?" in *Horizons in Hermeneutics*. For discussion of various practical applications of theological interpretation, see Porter, "What Difference Does Hermeneutics Make? Hermeneutical Theory Applied," Jian Dao 34/Pastoral Journal 27 (July 2010): 1-50. For another approach to the issues, see Grant Osborne, "Hermeneutics and Theological Interpretation," in *Understanding the Times: New Testament Studies in the 21st Century: Essays in Honor of D. A. Carson on the Occasion of His 65th Birthday*, ed. Andreas J. Köstenberger and Robert W. Yarbrough (Wheaton, IL: Crossway, 2011), pp. 62-86.

noted above, the general dissatisfaction with so-called historical criticism—even though historical criticism keeps recurring in various treatments (and is highly prized by a number of theological interpreters). A second is the usually positive, though sometimes qualified, view of premodern (or sometimes called precritical) interpretation, especially as represented and encapsulated in the rule of faith. A third is the significant role of the interpretive community, especially identified as the Christian church. A fourth is the ambiguous role, though not always clearly stated, of the Holy Spirit in the interpretive process. A fifth is the relationship of theological interpretation to general and special hermeneutics, where there is a difference of opinion on this relationship. A sixth and final idea that finds its way regularly into the discussion is the question of whether theological interpretation is a method or not.

There are a number of observations to be made about these features of theological interpretation. The first is that, despite its common origins in theological hermeneutics—I realize that some might argue against this—discussion of this commonality is virtually absent from the major characteristics of the movement, so that much discussion is often nonhermeneutical and nonphilosophical. Only in the fifth tenet noted above—the relationship of theological hermeneutics to general and special hermeneutics, where there is disagreement among advocates—is there the hint of its roots in theological hermeneutics. One of the major proponents of theological hermeneutics, who has been exalted by some as the major figure in theological interpretation, Kevin Vanhoozer, has written two major works that advocate for general and special hermeneutics respectively. With his acolyte, Daniel Treier, Vanhoozer wishes to keep discussion of both general and special hermeneutics alive.[12] Not all have followed them in this interest. As a result,

---

[12]Kevin J. Vanhoozer, *Is There a Meaning in This Text? The Bible, the Reader, and the Morality of Literary Knowledge* (Grand Rapids: Zondervan, 1998); idem, *The Drama of Doctrine: A Canonical-Linguistic Approach to Christian Theology* (Louisville: Westminster John Knox, 2005); Daniel J. Treier, *Introducing Theological Interpretation of Scripture: Recovering a Christian Practice* (Grand Rapids: Baker, 2008), pp. 127-56.

the level of direct hermeneutical engagement evident in these advocates is often limited. In fact, I would say that, for many of them, their groundedness in premodern interpretation virtually excludes significant interaction with recent hermeneutical thought, with Stephen Fowl going so far as to want to distance theological interpretation from any general hermeneutics.[13] Speech-act theory, used by major advocates of theoretical hermeneutics, is not a major component of theological interpretation. While Treier wishes, again following his teacher, to defend speech-act philosophy as a means of ensuring certain theological concerns, Fowl calls into question the use of speech-act theory, because he believes it is only useful to address a set of specific problems of language and meaning instead of constituting the basis of a general theory of language.[14] The issue of biblical hermeneutics constituting a generalized (or perhaps better biblicized) special hermeneutic is not raised in a significant way. Thus at this point theological interpretation does not address the issues of theological or biblical hermeneutics.

The second observation is that theological interpretation has tended to cross from concern for understanding of texts to become, at least in many instances of practice if not by all of the advocates themselves, a purported method of interpretation.[15] The fact that it is widely discussed whether theological interpretation is a method conforms with the further fact that there are plenty of instances of those who are using it as a means of interpretation. On that grounds alone, theological interpretation is not a hermeneutic so much as a technique (to use a Gadamerian distinction), and not even a theological hermeneutic but a means of theological interpretation. However, this

---

[13]Stephen E. Fowl, *Theological Interpretation of Scripture* (Eugene, OR: Cascade, 2009), pp. 37-40.

[14]Fowl, *Theological Interpretation*, pp. 47-48. Cf. Treier, *Introducing Theological Interpretation*, pp. 142-45; J. Todd Billings, *The Word of God for the People of God: An Entryway to the Theological Interpretation of Scripture* (Grand Rapids: Eerdmans, 2010), pp. 31-70.

[15]Cf. Joel B. Green, *Seized by Truth: Reading the Bible as Scripture* (Nashville: Abingdon, 2007), pp. 103-41 on method; with idem, *Practicing Theological Interpretation: Engaging Biblical Texts for Faith and Formation* (Grand Rapids: Baker, 2011), pp. 127-28 and *passim*.

practice is itself highly problematic, because once one even cursorily explores the range of interpretations offered under this rubric, it becomes clear that theological interpretation is not a method in the singular, not even methods in the plural, but a wide-ranging variety of types of theological interpretation (I consciously still use this term as an umbrella term for what I have discovered). Some of these are grammatical historical in nature, while others are higher critical. Some are canonical, while others are literalistic. Some dwell upon the premodern interpreters, while others are rhetorical.[16] If theological interpretation is a method, it does not appear to be a coherent method, but one that lacks a coherent methodological center. In any case, the fact that it has become more of an invocation of interpretations influenced in some way or another by premodern or precritical interpreters makes clear that it does not constitute the basis of a responsible theological or biblical hermeneutic.

The third observation is that there is ambiguity regarding the role of premodern or precritical interpretation. This ambiguity is seen in a number of different ways. The first is in defining its role. Is it determinative, normative or merely instructive? I think it varies considerably among both advocates and practitioners. Appeal is often made to the rule of faith or particular early creeds as guides to theological interpretation, with the idea that the normative doctrinal belief of the church is foundational. The problem here, however, is that whereas this may present some kind of interpretive or even hermeneutical parameters, it cannot constitute guidance for developing a method of interpretation or sustained or detailed interpretation. The hard work of exegesis is still required, which is evidenced in the widely varying methods actually used in what are purported to be instances of theological interpretation. There is the further issue of what reliance upon premodern interpreters does to further interpretation. Does it mean that new interpretations are

---

[16]I am sure that some of those would be surprised to find their essays represented as theological interpretation in Stephen E. Fowl, ed., *The Theological Interpretation of Scripture: Classic and Contemporary Readings* (Oxford: Blackwell, 1997).

excluded because they are not envisioned by these earlier interpreters? Some advocates of theological interpretation apparently wish to bring modern conceptions of interpretation into dialogue with premodern interpretation, but it is unclear, at least to me, how this can profitably occur, without some type of larger interpretive construct to adjudicate, for example, when ancient conceptions of the person conflict with modern conceptions of the person (to take merely one example).[17] Simply invoking the idea of figural or nonliteral reading does not suffice.[18] Further, it is not clear, at least to me, why it is that premodern interpretation is privileged. It appears in some instances that it is privileged simply because it is premodern and precritical. I agree that there are potential serious limitations to post-Enlightenment interpretation. Post-Enlightenment interpretation is subject to its own cultural, scientific, social and other presuppositions. Many of these have been too readily accepted, and there has been too much willing embrace of contemporary constructs, rather than holding them with the suspicion that is required. We have certainly seen this in modern science, where the Newtonian world gave way to the mechanistic universe, only to be confounded by the Einsteinian and quantum world of today. However, the premodern interpreters were themselves subject to the same types of presuppositions and constraints as we are—except that they were the ones of their age. Finally, what do we do when we realize that the ancients were simply wrong? I would argue that premodern or precritical interpreters, rather than following the teaching of Jesus and of Paul in a number of areas, rejected them and hence took the church in directions it should not have gone, such as restricting the roles of women, continuing to participate in such social evils as slavery and forming too close an alliance with government especially after the conversion of Constantine. I do not believe that theological interpretation has ade-

---

[17]See Green, *Practicing Theological Interpretation*, pp. 81-85, where it appears that Green puts modern neuroscience at the same level as Scripture, insofar as validating understanding is concerned.

[18]See Fowl, *Theological Interpretation*, pp. 56-63.

quately addressed such issues and how they relate to wider questions of interpretation—such as how to adjudicate among readings in light of historical contingency and anomaly, how to maintain continuity in Christian theological tradition while also allowing for new and productive interpretations to emerge, and how to differentiate fundamental from nonfundamental doctrine.

The fourth observation is that there is a clear tension within theological interpretation over the relationship between premodern interpretation and the modern interpreting community, that is, the church. One of the significant recent developments both within Christian thought and in hermeneutical and interpretive thought is the notion of community. The role of the Christian community and the need for communal activity has had a resurgence of interest within Christian circles. Some would say that this is generationally motivated as an emerging generation rebels against the flaunted rugged individualism and every-person-for-himself attitude of a previous generation. Others would say that this is the result of an embattled Christianity that no longer enjoys the suasion that it once did in contemporary society. Others would perhaps say that it is one of the products of postmodernism, as various tribes congregate around one another as self-identified communities coexisting with other competing communities. Of course, there is also the possibility that this is reflective of a desirable model of Christian formation and existence. Whatever the case, the fundamental role of the Christian ecclesial community is one of the tenets of theological interpretation. This tendency is clearly related to the notion of alignment with premodern interpretation, in that the modern Christian community is seen to be consonant with the body of belief of previous generations, rather than promoting the kind of new (and destructive) interpretations that emerged with Enlightenment thought and the role of individualism. Pragmatic forms of criticism, such as types of reader-response criticism and neopragmatism, have also emphasized the role of the community of interpreters. They, however, have not necessarily aligned themselves with previous traditions of interpretation, but have used communities as a way of validating interpretation. Nevertheless, there is a sense of continuity, because any new interpretation must recruit or find its own fellow interpreters if it wishes to constitute an interpreting community. Thus, many communities of interpreters practice intrinsic criticism by gathering around and modifying previous interpretations. Those who tend to interpret texts in the same way tend to congregate (figuratively, if not literally) with similar interpreters, and hence carry on their own discussions within the confines of their understanding of the text. This raises the question of what exactly is the nature of the modern interpretive community, and what are its relationships with previous interpreters. There are a number of possible alternatives. One is that communal interpretation endorses or validates previous interpretation. This raises questions regarding the place and possibility of new interpretations. Is interpretation simply meant to reinforce previous interpretation, or does it function within parameters set by previous interpretation, or is there a place for new interpretation, even if it is counter to such interpretation? I think that we must continue to be open to new interpretations and new understandings. Otherwise, our task is done.

The fifth observation concerns the reactionary emphasis upon premodern interpretation. The hermeneutical task, as defined above, is to find a means of answering two questions concerning the meaning of the original text and of the text for today. One of the major advances of philosophical hermeneutics incorporated into theological hermeneutics is the role that tradition plays in interpretation. There are lines of continuity that connect previous interpreters with previous interpreters. A useful analogy is found in the realm of music. Beethoven's *Appassionata* sonata was at one time considered a clangorous and avant-garde piece of music, only playable by the elite.[19] Today, one may readily hear this piece played as mainstream reper-

---

[19]I note that Westphal ("Philosophical/Theological View," p. 83) also uses this musical piece as an example, but we use it in different ways.

toire even by young pianists performing in competitions. The piece itself has not gotten easier, nor are pianists any stronger, faster, more agile than their predecessors. However, they have benefited from how interpretation of this musical piece has become part of the piano tradition, and they are interpreters who stand at the end of an accumulated weight of interpretive significance. I think that hermeneutical thought drives us to interpret in a similar way, knowing, appreciating and respecting those who have gone before us, while also being ready to explore new avenues as they open up to us. (I think also we could say that advances in recording technology have also led to an increased number of homogenized recordings, as interpreters are fearful of moving too far from the center of the tradition—again a useful parallel with contemporary theology.) There are some noteworthy exceptions, as already noted, but the emphasis on premodern interpretation at the expense of later interpretation runs the risk of overlooking all that has been learned in centuries of theological and biblical-critical and reflective thought. In some cases, the invocation of the past at the expense of the present resembles the reactionary tendencies found in ancient instrument enthusiasts (so-called authentic performance) or King James Bible advocates. They are trying to recapture a lost past but fail to realize that they themselves are situated within their own present, and they cannot recapture nor should they seek to revitalize previous interpretation, as if it fulfills the hermeneutical task.

These points of criticism show, I believe, that theological interpretation is not the way forward in developing theological responsibility in biblical hermeneutics. In fact, I believe that theological interpretation runs the risk of jeopardizing what it means to be a responsible biblical hermeneut, by attempting to overlook or negate, whether consciously or not, a biblical hermeneutic. It seems to me that theological interpretation has circumvented the hermeneutical process and with it the interpretive process, by advocating for a jumbled mix of contradictory proposals.

THEOLOGICAL RESPONSIBILITY AND
THE HERMENEUTICAL TASK

So, what is theological responsibility in light of the hermeneutical task? I think we first need to decide what theological responsibility is. The term is potentially—and perhaps rightly and intentionally—ambiguous, in a way that helps us to think more expansively about the concept. I think that theological responsibility implies responsibility on several different levels: being responsible to our theological heritage, being responsible when we do theology, being responsible for our theology as hermeneuts and interpreters, having theology play a guiding, responsible role in the hermeneutical enterprise, and, finally, recognizing that biblical hermeneutics has a theological responsibility.[20]

We cannot pretend that we do not have a theological heritage that has been instrumental and formative in establishing, perpetuating and even regulating our theological tradition. We cannot nor should not abandon such a heritage, even if we come to believe that some of the things that were advocated in the past have perhaps been unhelpful or even wrong. Self-criticism and correction has always been a part of the Christian tradition at its best. The Christian theological tradition is a strong one that has benefited from robust critical engagement from its inception (I happen to think that the label precritical is a misnomer for premodern criticism, because it was critical in its own way, just not necessarily skeptical). From Pauline exegesis of the Old Testament to the present, there has been a continuing tradition of interpretation and reinterpretation of the Christian texts and their resulting theology, and we must and should embrace this heritage of theology and interpretation (e.g., during the several Reformations, nineteenth-century social activism, etc.). Such a tradition imposes a burden upon us to be responsible interpreters when we engage in the theological task, whether as exegetes of Scripture, as biblical theologians or as systematic theolo-

---

[20]See Anthony C. Thiselton, *The Hermeneutics of Doctrine* (Grand Rapid: Eerdmans, 2007), as an exemplification of the bringing together of hermeneutics and doctrine in instructive and responsible ways.

gians. Theology in its various forms, with each generation subsequently standing on the shoulders of the previous generation, requires that we know and appreciate, even if we disagree with, the previous interpretation, always returning to our primary sources but acknowledging that their interpretation is influenced by and the result of others who have engaged in similar acts of reading and understanding. One of the shortcomings of theological interpretation, I believe, is its failure to understand the reception history of biblical and theological interpretation. Certain interpreters, especially those of the premodern period, and even certain periods in the life of the church (such as the fourth and fifth centuries with the development of the major creeds), are in effect stripped of their historical, temporal and sociopolitical embeddedness and repristinated as timeless doctrine to be considered on the same level—or on even a higher level, because they have synthesized, codified and generalized away the peculiarities—as the scriptural texts themselves. Theological interpretation does not recognize that each formulation or period of previous interpretation stands as one diachronic slice along a progression of interpretation. We must recognize with due respect those who have come before us, and wear the burden of further interpretation heavily, but we cannot avoid this responsibility as interpreters. In this way, our previous interpretation serves as an important formative influence and constant guide as we continue the process of interpretation—learning from both the productive interpretations and unfortunate errors of previous interpreters as we continue to engage the Bible as our primary text and the basis of our interpretations. In this way, our theological hermeneutics brings the two horizons of our theology—the original formulation as found in the text and the current understanding—into meaningful dialogue.

Hermeneutics, and especially biblical hermeneutics, can clearly help us in this task. Rather than marginalizing biblical interpretation as primarily a reactive theological enterprise, or treating it as an adjunctive enterprise in relation to general or special hermeneutics, I think that biblical hermeneutics addresses directly our major challenges to Christian theology. First, it allows us to focus upon the text of the Bible, as the primary source of our analysis and understanding. Perhaps even more importantly, it makes us realize that all of our interpretive methods—even those that claim to be getting us back to the original text (whether these are forms of historical criticism or types of literary criticism or linguistic criticism)—have their preunderstandings and preconditions of understanding, are culturally, historically and temporally embedded, and are themselves the reflections of developing thought about what it means to understand especially through language. Second, it allows us to recognize the role of the author in interpretation, even if it is to realize that notions of authorship are themselves highly complex. The notion of the author is one problematized by communal dimensions, composite assemblage, redactional activity over time, multiple versions, debates over personhood and differentiation, and legal issues. Their motivations and intentions are highly complex and not easily discernible, apart from the meanings that they have functionally realized in the language of their texts. Third, it embraces the significance of the reader as part of a developing and ongoing community of interpreters who utilize and refine various methods, debate the validity of their readings, appreciate the accumulated knowledge of the past, acknowledge their own locatedness, and still venture to put forth interpretations of texts. The result is no doubt going to be one in which there is—whether we wish it or not—productive plurality (though not necessarily relativity) of understanding, rather than the imposition of univocity.

CONCLUSION

I wish to conclude by simply affirming what I take to be an important intersection of thought and practice, exemplified by the one who first inspired this collection of essays, Professor Thiselton. He has made biblical hermeneutics his life's work. I am speculating here, but I think that some fellow New Testament scholars probably thought that he was wasting much of his time, if not much of his career, dabbling in esoteric terminology and reading complex writings dealing with what appeared to be abstract and arcane ideas—while they were simply getting down to work and exegeting texts and doing theology. How wrong they were. No one exegetes a text or does theology without being a participant, knowingly or not, in the hermeneutical task. Some are informed participants, while others simply unreflectively mimic the technique that they were taught—usually represented as some form of "objective" interpretation that is supposed to result in "factual" conclusions. Whereas for many, biblical interpretation, even sometimes called hermeneutics, is interpretation as technique, for Professor Thiselton biblical interpretation has always involved coming to terms first with biblical hermeneutics, that is, gaining an informed knowledge of what it means to understand the texts that are foundational to Christianity, in all of their philosophical and theological complexity. A robust hermeneutical approach, especially what I would call a theological hermeneutics that is attentive to our theological tradition and responsive to it in new and creative ways, is, I believe, essential to developing a theological responsibility and helping to guarantee a future for biblical interpretation. I wish to thank Professor Thiselton for doing so much to help all of us to at least have the opportunity and possibility of glimpsing what this future might be like through his own life and work.

3

Biblical Hermeneutics
and *Scriptural* Responsibility

Richard S. Briggs

I TAKE AS MY FOCAL QUESTION: what does it mean to wrestle with the reality of hermeneutical plurality while being responsible to Scripture? This question presupposes a ruling out of the two opposite ends of a possible spectrum. On the one hand we shall not deny the reality of hermeneutical plurality. Biblical interpretation is not the pursuit of a hard-won univocal set of results following from a correct understanding of how the Bible is (or is to be) interpreted. On the other hand, we shall assume the meaningfulness of a concept of responsibility to Scripture: the recognition of hermeneutical plurality does not mean that "anything goes" such that the voice of Scripture is nothing but the prejudice of the interpreter writ large. Both of these extreme positions have long track records across the theological spectrum, and are often easier to articulate than the kinds of middle-ground options that we will be pursuing here—where Scripture has a voice, while interpretative approaches are multiple and varied, with the results being a range of interpretations and practices characteristic of a range of Christian (and, differently, Jewish) theological convictions.[1]

Many writers have argued convincingly that the choice of interpretative practices that make sense with respect to Scripture is determined in significant ways by a network of assumptions and convictions about the nature and purpose of Scripture in the first place. This point has been made in both hermeneutical and theological terms.[2] One can of course pursue a more general theoretical discussion about how texts are read—general hermeneutics in the sense of mapping what Anthony Thiselton so helpfully describes as "the commitments and the responsibilities that are entailed in extra-linguistic terms"[3]—or one can even attempt to say how texts *should* be read in general, except that the broad category of text seems to be so vast and so multifaceted that one cannot proceed a great deal further than generalities about balancing attention to various kinds of context or various kinds of social, cultural and historical location in which reading takes place as an embodied act. The point here is that normative criteria with respect to hermeneutical engagement can only really exist, in anything but the broadest terms, when there is a goal or purpose in view for the reading.

In this chapter I suggest that a helpful way to make progress here is to think through the notion of responsibility to Scripture as relating to a range of ways in which we *construe* Scripture *as* something.[4] Rather

---

[1]I restrict myself in this chapter to Christian readings and Christian theology, although the question of Christian responsibility to Jewish Scripture that is now also Christian Scripture will come up below.

[2]E.g., R. W. L. Moberly, *The Old Testament of the Old Testament: Patriarchal Narratives and Mosaic Yahwism*, Overtures to Biblical Theology (Minneapolis: Fortress, 1992), p. 2; or Stephen E. Fowl, *Theological Interpretation of Scripture*, Cascade Companions (Eugene, OR: Wipf & Stock, 2009), pp. 1-12.

[3]Anthony C. Thiselton, *New Horizons in Hermeneutics. The Theory and Practice of Transforming Biblical Reading* (London: HarperCollins, 1992), p. 617. He is talking about self-involving language in particular, but the point may be taken more generally.

[4]I thus navigate here between my own more philosophically orientated discussion of construal in Richard S. Briggs, *Words in Action: Speech Act Theory and Biblical Interpretation* (Edinburgh: T & T Clark, 2001), pp. 105-43, and the profound theological cataloguing of various significant construals in David H. Kelsey, *The Uses of Scripture in Recent Theology* (Philadelphia: Fortress, 1975). For brief analysis of Kelsey's very helpful work see *Words in Action*, p. 125.

than talking bluntly about what "Scripture is," in other words, we might
better learn to speak of "Scripture as" whenever we want to offer judgments or criteria regarding the responsible interpretation of Scripture.
We shall explore this claim in several steps: looking at a range of ways in
which Scripture might be construed; asking how to evaluate that range;
and then focusing on the question of letting diverse construals interact
constructively rather than as mutually exclusive alternatives. I conclude
by attempting to articulate some key theological construals that will aid
the interpreter who seeks responsibility to Scripture.

"Scripture As": A Spectrum of Construals

The shift from "is" to "as" represents, in my judgment, one of the most
fundamental hermeneutical contributions to reflection on the nature of
human interpretation of the world and texts around us. It is a shift that
takes place in the long shadow cast by Immanuel Kant's great attempts
to categorize existence: a shift that finds different but not incompatible
expression in the streams of Anglo-American analytic philosophy (after
Wittgenstein) and continental philosophy (after Heidegger). Garrett
Green, in one of the most sustained theological treatments of the matter,
offers the notion that it is the shift from Kant's "copula of judgement"
("is") to the "copula of imagination" ("as").[5] Under this rubric it finds
patient expression in the work of Paul Ricoeur, who in the 1970s attempted to map these issues with respect to the "is and is not" of metaphor, but in the 1980s favored the conceptuality of imagination to describe the hermeneutical adventure, as his work focused more on the
interpretation of narratives and other written texts. And on another day
it would be interesting to ask whether the real hermeneutical significance of this "is/as" shift has been obscured by its coinciding with the
arrival of the postmodern, and the somewhat ungenerous and often
unfocused debates that this occasions among those in disciplines such
as theology or biblical studies. The postmodern mood, at least arguably,

---

[5]Garrett Green, *Imagining God: Theology and the Religious Imagination* (San Francisco:
Harper & Row, 1989), p. 73; cf. his whole discussion on pp. 70-74.

blurs the huge significance of "as/is" into a vague sense of everything
being open to ideological and political spin, which is not untrue as far
as it goes, but is rather an occasional social consequence of what is going
on and not the fundamental point at stake.[6]

Let us consider a spectrum of ways in which Scripture is construed,
from the most minimally imaginative to the most maximally creative,
and ask what the notion of "responsibility to Scripture" looks like across
this spectrum.

(1) One could envisage responsibility to Scripture as responsibility
to it simply *as text*. This puts us on the end of the spectrum where we
might want to agree with Werner Jeanrond's claim that the interpreter
of the Bible (or any significant religious text) needs a theory of text (or
textuality) as a fundamental category of hermeneutical thinking.[7] In
general terms it seems likely that a theory of textuality will not get us
very far in thinking about responsibility to Scripture *per se*, which is not
to say that textualization is not itself an interesting category within
Scripture for thinking about how traditions are passed down and maintained. How faith in Israel's God became articulated (and thereby potentially transformed) in written texts is currently a major focus of Old
Testament studies,[8] just as it is significant to recognize that the Corin-
thian correspondence offers something of "a correspondence course in
practical . . . hermeneutics" just because Paul was, in Margaret Mitchell's
terms, "the first Christian lexicographer, crafting a language" for early
Christian believers, but also working "to move those terms into sen-

---

[6]On such another occasion one would be well served by beginning with Anthony Thiselton's
patient explorations of the ways in which hermeneutical philosophy is and is not congruent
with the claims of leading postmodern theorists: see especially part VI of his *Thiselton on
Hermeneutics. The Collected Works and New Essays of Anthony Thiselton* (Aldershot, UK:
Ashgate, 2006), pp. 523-682.

[7]Werner G. Jeanrond, *Text and Interpretation as Categories of Theological Thinking* (New
York: Crossroad, 1988), programmatically on p. 73, but throughout.

[8]See, for example, William M. Schniedewind, *How the Bible Became a Book: The Textualization of Ancient Israel* (Cambridge: Cambridge University Press, 2004); and David M. Carr,
Writing on the Tablet of the Heart: Origins of Scripture and Literature (Oxford: Oxford University Press, 2005).

tences and paragraphs."[9] One productive focal point of hermeneutical reflection upon Scripture is therefore textuality, in terms of how written texts may or may not capture, mediate or recast what is at stake in experience of God, but this does not equate to saying that we need to understand what textuality is before we can handle Scripture responsibly.

It is also relevant to point out that this whole discussion of *Scripture as text* is related to, though framed differently from, the post–Brevard Childs discussion of what it means to read the Bible *as Scripture* rather than just as inert text on the page. This was of course one of Childs's fundamental concerns: to read the Old Testament *as* Scripture, as the hugely significant title of his 1979 book put it.[10] Here instead we would be taking the notion of Scripture as the given, and asking how that might in turn be construed. Thus this first category is in some senses simply a reversal of Childs's move, and as such, I would argue, it is headed in precisely the wrong direction.

(2) Only slightly further along the spectrum, and possibly representing the "Scripture is" default position among interpreters of the modern age, we have Scripture construed as a bearer of meaning. Scripture is still basically text, on this understanding, but text understood *as* in some sense assertion or proposition (or collections thereof). Debates about meaning are some of the most familiar hermeneutical discussions in biblical studies—by which I mean not debates about whether text *X* means *A* or *B*, but hermeneutical debates about what constitutes meaning with respect to biblical texts. Note that here again we are up against construal: whether authorial intention counts as meaning; or whether intertextual resonance counts as meaning; or whether traditions of reception count as meaning, and so forth.

I have discussed elsewhere the significance and limitations of working with meaning in biblical hermeneutics.[11] My own view is that meaning

---

[9]Margaret M. Mitchell, *Paul, the Corinthians and the Birth of Christian Hermeneutics* (Cambridge: Cambridge University Press, 2010), pp. 5, 16.

[10]Brevard S. Childs, *Introduction to the Old Testament as Scripture* (London: SCM, 1979).

[11]Richard S. Briggs, "How to Do Things with Meaning in Biblical Interpretation," *Southeastern Theological Review* 2 (2011): 143-60.

remains a useful tool with respect to specific words and phrases, but not with respect to conceptual categories (such as intention) or broader stretches of discourse. The theoretical discussion about meaning is thus largely unhelpful, while questions about the meaning of specific words (the example I take is *lo' tirtsach*, "do not kill/murder," in the Ten Commandments) remain not just helpful but essential. Philosophers may note that this argument is precisely that of J. L. Austin in his widely overlooked article "The Meaning of a Word."[12]

For a while, a few years ago, it was common for defenders of meaning to appeal to Kevin Vanhoozer's weighty project *Is There a Meaning in This Text?* to defend the notion that Scripture as bearer of meaning was what it was all about.[13] This book was in turn often construed as a treatise about biblical interpretation, whereas it was at least intending to be a theological account of the ontology of texts and the concomitant responsibilities of readers. It thus bears reflection that when Vanhoozer went on to discuss scriptural texts as communicative acts,[14] he was able to reframe the whole argument, which was congruent with his 1998 book, without reference to meaning, as his sometime interlocutor Stephen Fowl might indeed have anticipated he would be able to.[15] All of which brings us to:

(3) A more performatively orientated analysis, which argues that responsibility to Scripture is responsibility to Scripture construed *as* some functional communicative act: be it divine address, historical document, record of the testimonies of the faithful, partisan ideological

---

[12]J. L. Austin, "The Meaning of a Word," originally written in 1940, now available in his *Philosophical Papers*, 3rd ed. (Oxford: Clarendon Press, 1979), pp. 55-75.

[13]Kevin J. Vanhoozer, *Is There a Meaning in This Text? The Bible, the Reader, and the Morality of Literary Knowledge* (Grand Rapids: Eerdmans, 1998).

[14]Most notably in Kevin J. Vanhoozer, "From Speech Acts to Scripture Acts: The Covenant of Discourse and the Discourse of the Covenant," in his *First Theology: God, Scripture and Hermeneutics* (Downers Grove, IL: IVP Academic, 2002), pp. 159-203.

[15]See Briggs, "Meaning," pp. 151-55, for a review of the issues. The ways in which Vanhoozer's and Fowl's positions address the key issues are helpfully mapped by D. Christopher Spinks, *The Bible and the Crisis of Meaning: Debates on the Theological Interpretation of Scripture* (London and New York: T & T Clark, 2007).

construct ... one can, I think, see that this could be a long list. Here we finally arrive at the point that Scripture is always Scripture with a view; that hermeneutical approaches need to be measured against the overarching goals of why Scripture is being read. Clearly, in broad terms, a reader whose concern is deeper adoration of the triune God is unlikely to be asking the same interpretative questions of John's Gospel as a reader whose concern is with tracing the stratifications of community disputes in and out of first-century synagogues. Perhaps the most lively form of discussion about this kind of interpretative diversity today concerns what, if anything, demarcates a specifically theological form of construal of Scripture, such that one might have a practice of theological interpretation of Scripture which can be differentiated from other kinds of interpretation. This is not a straightforward matter to adjudicate, as the proliferation of manifestoes and overviews and proposals pertaining to this matter (both for and against) testifies.[16]

(4) Perhaps one can go further, and suggest that there are ways of construing Scripture that self-consciously and deliberately step outside of Scripture's own self-presenting categories, and which hold no concern for such a construal being a communicative act. Rather, one might make of Scripture what one will, with no interest in whether such readings could plausibly be traced back any further than the imagination of today's reader. This can happen in various ways: among the deliberately playful ironies of freewheeling postmodern theorists (such as, for example, the interestingly titled *The New Testament as True Fiction*[17]); among the angry who are determined only to show the incoherence of theistic claims; and among the would-be spiritual who feel that the Lord has spoken directly to them, in rather unmediated fashion, about how the text is to be construed today. In some ways I wonder if these self-

---

[16]Fowl, *Theological Interpretation*, pp. 76-88, offers a very useful annotated bibliography. We shall come to one way of articulating what makes for theological interpretation below.

[17]Douglas A. Templeton, *The New Testament as True Fiction: Literature, Literary Criticism, Aesthetics*, Playing the Texts 3 (Sheffield, UK: Sheffield Academic Press, 1999). Note both the "as" in the title, and the name of the (short-lived) series in which it appeared: "playing the texts."

sufficient construals are extreme forms of performative construal, as per (3) above, possibly as exercises in making what one will of what Eco famously called "open works," by which, initially at least, he meant to refer to works of modern art that had little interest in directing the communicative act.[18] In any case, fascinating though such instances may be, they are not our focus here, since any hermeneutical responsibility, such as it is, is not to Scripture in such cases, but to some other agenda (be it ethical, aesthetic, spiritual or whatever).

These, then, are several positions spread out along the spectrum: Scripture as text; Scripture as bearer of meaning; Scripture as communicative act (or as grouping of several communicative acts); Scripture as raw data for interpretative free play (or possibly hermeneutical will-to-power). What is most helpful in the first two categories is to some extent a special set of limiting cases of the third. Thus it is with respect to this third category that we press on to ask the question about how to evaluate divergent construals.

EVALUATING DIVERGENT CONSTRUALS: ORIENTATIONS AND OPTIONS

How then should one evaluate the hermeneutical issues raised by saying that Scripture is always *Scripture as*? There are a large number of variables to consider here, which should muster an appropriate caution about sweeping statements in this regard. I will offer two broad observations by way of orientation, and then separate out three options for thinking about what to do with the diversity.

(1) *Different biblical texts operate differently, but all of them are indeed part of the one (holy, catholic and apostolic) scriptural text.* Each pole of this observation can be so emphasized by some that the other pole is

---

[18]Eco's earliest (1962) work in this area was only translated into English in 1989 as *The Open Work* (Cambridge, MA: Harvard University Press, 1989), by which time his work on semiotics and texts was well known. This possibly rather muddles the English-language perception of how much Eco's idea of an "open work" was originally a theory about written texts in particular. Initially, at least, it was not.

lost from sight. I do wonder whether the emphasis one chooses depends sometimes on the overemphasis against which one is reacting. Thus the rise of modern critical impulses seems to have been fueled in part by frustration with an overly pious insistence on the immunity of holy Scripture from criticism: if doctrine forecloses on textual investigation, then hermeneutics urges that doctrine be deemphasized to make way for the text, which is characteristic of hermeneutical traditions indebted to Schleiermacher. On the other hand, if one is immersed in the details of text after text in its originating cultural and historical specificity and one never arrives at the moment of asking what brought such texts together in the canonical collection such that they might be maintained for readers far removed from that originating context—well, then, the rise of anxiety over the potential barrenness of such reading can be well understood, by, say, a theologically inclined pastor preaching in Safenwil in 1917.[19] It will be interesting to ask, in a moment, what might happen were one to attempt to articulate this tension without overreaction, and without simply saying there are lots of different cases to consider.

(2) *Different hermeneutical approaches result in different types of interpretation seeming plausible.* This is arguably one of the great contributions of Jauss to the study of reception history, following his teacher Gadamer, and emphasizing that the horizons of plausibility in interpretation are shaped (though not entirely determined) by the past and ongoing reception of the text. In Ulrich Luz's felicitous image, the interpreter is in a boat on the river of tradition, implicated in the ongoing interpretative trajectory of the tradition, and able to steer forward in a (small) variety of directions, but always from a particular point, with particular questions that make sense as the live ones to ask.[20]

---

[19]And thus Karl Barth on "The Strange New World Within the Bible," in his *The Word of God and the Word of Man* (London: Hodder & Stoughton, 1928), pp. 28-50; now retranslated by Amy Marga as "The New World in the Bible," in *The Word of God and Theology* (New York: Continuum, 2011), pp. 15-29. Barth was a pastor for ten years in Safenwil, although the "strange new world" piece was in fact preached in the church at nearby Leutwil (and, according to Marga, in February 1917, "New World," p. 15).

[20]Cf. Ulrich Luz, *Matthew in History: Interpretation, Influence, and Effects* (Minneapolis:

I take it that this kind of observation brings us to one central instantiation of the hermeneutical plurality of which we are speaking today. Different interpreters at different times simply do have different goals, and while some interpretations may be ruled deficient in that they do not attend to the actual details of the text (or perhaps misread them as something other), many of the interpretative disputes that actually occupy anyone's time are not over such matters, but over competing construals of the nature of the text's purpose and specific contribution to that purpose. Few such construals are ever impossible. Again it will be interesting to ask, in a moment, what positive conclusions might follow from such a diversity.

The question before us, then, is this: Given that different construals of Scripture are possible, as just noted, how does one evaluate that diversity? Let us consider three options.

(1) In the first instance one might pursue the argument that in fact only one such construal is correct. Perhaps an interpreter wants to affirm that Scripture really is divine promise in a way that it is not also partisan politics (or again, vice versa). For some, Scripture is about making true statements concerning what happened; or truly revealing the nature of God; or truly narrating the story of Israel, Christ and the church. One could put names to some of these proposals, and one could, I think, often find adherents of one or another proposal who do not accept that any other construal of Scripture is plausible, worthwhile or correct. As A. K. M. Adam has pointed out, it is in fact rare to find interpreters working on this model who give any thought at all to the hermeneutical implications of supposing that only one construal is correct.[21] The implications include that most interpreters are wrong most of the time, and that the average Bible reader may well have no

---

Fortress, 1994), especially p. 25; drawing on the work of Gadamer and Jauss. For an excellent discussion of this whole area, see David Paul Parris, *Reception Theory and Biblical Hermeneutics*, Princeton Theological Monograph Series (Eugene, OR: Pickwick, 2009).

[21]See A. K. M. Adam, "Integral and Differential Hermeneutics," in his *Faithful Interpretation: Reading the Bible in a Postmodern World* (Minneapolis: Fortress, 2006), pp. 81-103, especially pp. 93-95 on "respectful dissent."

way of adjudicating disagreement among interpreters, other than hoping that they back the right expert. The prospects, on such a model, seem dispiriting.

(2) In the second instance, one could import the spirit of the cultural revolution into biblical studies and let a thousand construals bloom. Some textbooks give this impression: offering a broad array of reading strategies attached to different construals of the purpose of Scripture, and suggesting, whether explicitly or implicitly by the arrangement of the book, that it all depends on what you happen to be interested in. A chapter for feminists; a chapter for vegetarians; a chapter then also for Methodists, or Mormons, or Marxists . . . and then one can begin to see that what looks like hermeneutical hospitality to all ends up being unlikely to allow the claims of any to be aired on their own terms. Rather significantly, responsibility to the text has dropped out of the picture completely, to be replaced by exercises in cutting the text to suit more or less any interpretative agenda. And in any case, the cultural revolution is probably a somewhat unhopeful model for real progress.

(3) A third option, which I have left to the last because it is the one I want to advocate, is that a truly hermeneutical way with the diversity of construals is to bring them into productive conversation one with another, and look to see what can be learned from what we might call an integrated hermeneutical approach to the reading of Scripture.[22] Responsibility to the text reappears in this case because as soon as you have two contrasting construals of the text—of both its purpose and specific contribution—a sort of triangulating effect sets in whereby Methodists and Marxists, say, or Anglicans and atheists, might discuss together how it is that they see one and the same set of words in such different ways.[23]

It is admittedly more common to see people respond to the diversity

---

[22]Cf. Adam's use of "integral" in the article cited in note 21. My argument here is not unrelated to Adam's proposal, though the multiplicity of perspectives on his account is generated by textual underdetermination, whereas I am urging that texts may be determined to all kinds of varying degrees but the key is that the framing construals can be so different.

[23]I am sure that the sets of "Marxist Methodists" and "Atheist Anglicans" are not empty ones, but it will suffice that they are small.

of construals of Scripture by falling back either to option one, where one construal is urged to the exclusion of others (thus "it really is about a Marxist process of trickling into the land" or "it really is about holy war" or "it really is a morally reprehensible exercise in self-legitimation"); or option two, where one tries to say that any model might have its merits and who are we to say . . . The notion that hermeneutics is about fostering dialogue between competing claims to the scriptural text does, I suppose, sit better with certain understandings of life before God than others. It will work well for those for whom it is possible to imagine that such a communal paradigm of holding together diversity in creative tension makes for a better vision of human flourishing before God, rather than thinking that the key is to resolve it all in favor of the correct way ahead. Rowan Williams has suggested that such a vision is in a sense a profoundly Anglican one.[24] Maybe, therefore, I am advocating an Anglican response to hermeneutical plurality and scriptural responsibility, which may perhaps be appropriate in light of the honoree of this volume! Be that as it may, I do think it is a profoundly hermeneutical response.

So, for example, some might consider that the task of taking the totality of all the different construals of Scripture and somehow holding them together in a creative tension seems unduly optimistic or naive when some of them seem so flatly to contradict other ones. What would it mean, for instance, to hold together the notion of Scripture as means of grace with Scripture as partisan self-deception? Yet no sooner is such an option articulated than one can begin to think of interesting ways in which divine grace might be operative in and through the mechanisms of human self-deception. It is neither a prerequisite nor a condition for divine grace that one extricate oneself from webs of self-deception, but rather among such struggles, and indeed occasionally through them, comes the working of

---

[24]The ability to maintain dialogue across contested traditions is a key (Anglican) point for Williams and is thus argued in many places. Possibly his most significant statement of the matter is in his 1998 Lambeth Conference paper, "On Making Moral Decisions," published as "Making Moral Decisions" in Robin Gill, ed., *The Cambridge Companion to Christian Ethics* (Cambridge: Cambridge University Press, 2001), pp. 3-15.

God in grace. Thus Joseph: "Even though you intended to do harm to me, God intended it for good" (Gen 50:20). Or rather than contrasting, on the one hand, historical reconstruction or the analysis of the social and political makeup of the text with, on the other, claims about the text's role in the divine economy as a form of revelation of the God of Scripture, it becomes urgent instead to see how one's understanding of God should be shaped by the fact that the text before us has come to be what it is in such particular historical, social and political ways.

So to take a relatively simple example, it is not difficult to track the ways in which the visionary hope and optimism of Second Isaiah is pursued in the canonical book of Isaiah by the concluding unspectacular postscript of Third Isaiah, beset as he (or it) is by sectarian infighting amongst the newly returned to Jerusalem. Now there are those who will only linger on the mountaintops with Second Isaiah and essay great theological claims directly out of its poetry. And there are those who will only turn to the grim sociopolitical realities of Third Isaiah and conjure a collapse of prophecy into the disarray of apocalyptic as a man turns against his fellow man, depending on each of their agendas with respect to land, priesthood, temple, sacrifice, ethnic exclusion and so on. But readers of Second Isaiah are not invited to stop at chapter 55, and no one is invited to take up and read only at chapter 56. Both of these construals of the Isaianic text are in some senses very persuasive. But the key is: neither is to be embraced without the other. Or perhaps, to be responsible to Scripture, we may say that proponents of one need to be able to see why the other has adherents too, and work toward articulating how the God of the book of Isaiah is to be better understood by holding the two together. Or at least that is the canonical invitation of the scriptural book of Isaiah.[25]

We have arrived, then, at the main thesis of this chapter, at least as stated in formal hermeneutical terms. That scriptural responsibility in the face of hermeneutical plurality is a responsibility to fostering dia-

---

[25]This example of course is derivative from Childs's celebrated overview of the book, *Introduction*, pp. 311-38.

logue between multiple competing construals of "*Scripture as*," arrayed across the domains of the theological, the literary, the historical, the cultural, the psychological and so forth. And furthermore, we might add, that within this broad understanding, one might then define *theological interpretation* as any interpretation which will make sure that theological construals are among those explicitly considered. Note that this does not prejudge the extent to which other critical perspectives will or will not be brought into play, and neither, at this stage, does it clarify actual theological content in any particular construal.

Thus in what remains of this chapter, I want to go on and sketch out some of the substantive theological/hermeneutical construals that I think are of most significance in taking Christian Scripture responsibly.

Substantive Scriptural Responsibility

Thus far I have tried to say as noncommittally as possible what counts hermeneutically as a way of holding together our key concerns. To make progress toward specifics, I want to set to one side those kinds of plurality that follow from deliberately cutting loose the scriptural text from playing a constructive role in Christian theological work. The kinds of plurality that celebrate, for instance, the creative hermeneutical accounting of a Stanley Fish, while they deserve their own proper discussion, would simply take us down a whole different set of paths at this point, and instead I want to focus on the kinds of construals that still proliferate even within approaches which seek to let Scripture play its constructive role. This is, I think, the theologically more interesting discussion: multiple construals that all fall within the canonical purview. I suggest that this phenomenon reflects one of the key functions of Scripture—to maintain the mysterious boundaries within which proper theological articulation can take place.

Indeed, because Scripture is always *Scripture as*, one could say that we are engaged as biblical interpreters and theologians in the search for the Christian Bible. This is one of the key claims of the complex and contested oeuvre of Brevard Childs. Scripture preserves the precise form of challenge and encouragement of attempting to discern the ways of God in and through human language, experience and tradition. It leaves us with a proper set of questions, and sets limits as to where we may turn for answers, but it does not give itself up easily to resolving the key issues that lie at the center of this range of theological issues: questions concerning divine action, human response and a whole range of theological *topoi* in between.[26] In terms of specifics, responsibility to Scripture might commit the Christian reader to the following construals of Scripture as particularly significant among all the others:

(1) The two-testament structure of Scripture is of paramount hermeneutical significance. Hermeneutical proposals that only work with the New Testament as sacred text will miss the complex issues that are raised by the nature and status of the Old Testament as Christian Scripture. Old Testament texts are sprung into canonical tension in ways that raise whole sets of questions about authors, intentions, meanings, reference and so forth that are hidden from view in more straightforward examples of significant texts, including the New Testament itself.[27]

(2) Scripture offers a complex interweaving of promise and judgment, as well as many other significant theological topics that are often held to be in fundamental tension. Many key theological convictions are shaped in such dialectical terms: divine sovereignty and human responsibility;[28] sin and forgiveness; inclusion and exclusion. Many of these tensions, it may be noted, arise from estimating differently the degrees of continuity and discontinuity between the Old and New Testament witnesses to the issue in question. One could illustrate this with

---

[26]It is not possible to pursue the question here of how to read Childs for this thesis; but see in particular Daniel Driver, *Brevard Childs, Biblical Theologian: For the Church's One Bible*, Forschungen zum Alten Testament 2/46 (Tübingen: Mohr Siebeck, 2010).

[27]This claim is one of the burdens of my contribution to the *Festschrift* for Anthony Thiselton: "'The Rock Was Christ': Paul's Reading of Numbers and the Significance of the Old Testament for Theological Hermeneutics," in Stanley E. Porter and Matthew Malcolm, eds., *Horizons in Hermeneutics* (Grand Rapids: Eerdmans, 2013).

[28]Note here the published PhD thesis of D. A. Carson, *Divine Sovereignty and Human Responsibility: Biblical Perspectives in Tension* (1981; repr., London: Marshall Pickering, 1994), where Carson thinks that "a fair treatment of the biblical data leaves the sovereignty-responsibility tension restless in our hands" (p. 220).

respect to differing convictions about church government: in what
senses do Old Testament notions of priesthood inform Christian
practice and a Christian theology of church leadership, and in what
senses are they to be understood as set aside? Different views of the law
in Lutheran and Calvinist traditions offer another obvious example. In
most such cases there seems little likelihood of arriving at one answer
that will compel all serious Christian thinkers to agree, and it may be
that a more realistic sense of fostering hermeneutical discussion between the competing claims might show that there is genuinely more
than one way of faithfully working out some of these issues.

(3) Scripture is in some fundamental sense a means of grace. While
grace and human response might be one further example of the dialectical tension between competing poles that we have just been considering, there is, I think, some key way in which Scripture is rightly construed as one means (among others) in which the grace of God is active
among human living. This is the positive half of William Abraham's
thesis about *Canon and Criterion*: that the great canons of the church
(which include Scripture, as well as sacraments, creeds, the fathers and
various others) are to be understood as means of grace rather than as
epistemological criteria.[29] With respect to Scripture, then, which becomes the focus of Abraham's account from the Reformers onward, for
obvious reasons, this involves taking *Scripture as* a means of grace. Reflecting on 2 Timothy 3, Abraham notes that it offers something of a
"modest proposal" for how to characterize Scripture (the Old Testament,
in this instance): it is "a gift from God" whose "fundamental purposes
... are soteriological, pedagogical, and pastoral."[30] Scripture may then be
paradigmatic for other canonical traditions, which are "best seen as
means of grace, as gifts of the Holy Spirit in the Church. They mediate
the life of God, bringing healing and salvation to the world."[31] The very

---

[29]William J. Abraham, *Canon and Criterion in Christian Theology* (Oxford: Oxford University
Press, 1998). The 2002 paperback reprint includes some response to critics of the book.
[30]Ibid., p. 51.
[31]Ibid., p. 52.

modesty of such a proposal mitigates against seeing Scripture then as an epistemological norm. Rather, "the canon of Scripture . . . is a body of literature inspired by God and adopted over time in the Church to make us wise unto salvation."[32] While it may be that Abraham unduly polarizes the choice between two construals that need not perhaps be in quite such irreconcilable tension, as some of his critics have suggested, he rightly insists that Scripture reaches forward to facilitate further theological work within the mysterious boundaries of the canon, rather than primarily functioning as a yardstick for resolving theological disputes. If divine grace is not being recognized in our work with the scriptural text, then perhaps we are no longer reading the Bible as Christian Scripture in certain important ways? That grace brings with it corresponding human summons and ethical responsibility need not be denied, but to recognize that the initiative lies with God may yet be hermeneutically productive. This leads us, more broadly, to consider the sense in which human texts are also divine communication:

(4) The fact that Scripture serves as divine revelation of the triune communicative God even while at the same time it consists of so many different genres of human interaction remains an important and productive matrix for understanding scriptural responsibility. This was argued above, in contrast to still-prevalent approaches that seek to play the one off against the other, from either side. Arguably the most probing examples of this intriguing hermeneutical interaction between divine and human speech are found in the Old Testament, specifically in the Psalms. Childs recognizes this canonical switch effected by Psalm 1 as a hermeneutical introduction to the Psalter, whereby the prayers of worshipers become the Word of God through a process of canonical textualization.[33] Dietrich Bonhoeffer famously averred that it is Christ who prays in the Psalms, and the extent to which he intended this as a reading strategy or as an ontological statement about

---

[32]Ibid., p. 477.
[33]Childs, *Introduction*, p. 513.

holy Scripture can be debated.[34] But it is, I think, undeniable that the average biblical commentator, even with faith commitments, has in the past century or two found it much easier to translate divine address into human communication rather than the other way around. Thus accounts of divine speech can be reconstrued as what the prophets or the apostles thought God meant, but the ways in which the articulations of the prophets and the apostles can in turn be understood as divine address have remained more mysterious and less probed. To borrow Kevin Vanhoozer's felicitous framework for analyzing this: we have been better at demythologization (across the theological spectrum, one might add) than at remythologization.[35] For Vanhoozer, the key hermeneutical mechanisms by which the sprawling diversity of human voices can be at one and the same time the communicative act of the God of Scripture are furnished by Mikhail Bakhtin's explorations of dialogical discourse.[36] I have suggested elsewhere that what Vanhoozer explores with regard to theological articulation might then be brought back to bear on the texts of Scripture itself with regard to divine speech, and thus that we might in this sense "remythologize Scripture" and find a way of understanding its human words as divine address.[37] Regardless of whether this particular way of negotiating the issues is a fruitful way ahead (and I think it is), we can still affirm that responsibility to Scripture in the face of hermeneutical plurality must involve com-

---

[34]Dietrich Bonhoeffer, *The Psalms: Prayer Book of the Bible* (orig. 1940; available in two different English translations: Oxford: SLG Press, 1982, as a pamphlet; or in *Dietrich Bonhoeffer Works, Vol. 5: Life Together and Prayerbook of the Bible: An Introduction to the Psalms* [Minneapolis: Fortress, 1996], pp. 155-77). Bonhoeffer's text is sufficiently brief that more than one interpretation may be plausible.

[35]Thus Kevin J. Vanhoozer, *Remythologizing Theology: Divine Action, Passion, and Authorship*, Cambridge Studies in Christian Doctrine 18 (Cambridge: Cambridge University Press, 2010).

[36]A key text is M. M. Bakhtin, *The Dialogical Imagination: Four Essays*, ed. Michael Hoquist (Austin, TX: University of Texas Press, 1981).

[37]Richard S. Briggs, "On 'Seeing' What God Is 'Saying': Rereading Biblical Narrative in Dialogue with Kevin Vanhoozer's *Remythologizing Theology*," in Roger Kojecký and Andrew Tate, eds., *Visions and Revisions: The Word and the Text* (Newcastle, UK: Cambridge Scholars Press, 2012).

mitment to holding together the elements of divine and human discourse that are found through the canon.

Here then are four specific theological construals of Scripture that might productively frame Christian wrestling with hermeneutical plurality: two testaments, in a creative set of theological tensions, as a means of grace, and held together dialogically as the communicative acts of the one God who is the God of Abraham, Isaac and Jacob, and also the God of our Lord Jesus Christ. There are of course many other theological commitments that the Christian reader of Scripture will have in mind during readings of the biblical text, and I have no desire to say that these four are necessarily primary, but they are all at least in some way focused quite directly on hermeneutical issues. And there are many other general hermeneutical commitments that such a reader will want to undertake as they would in handling any text responsibly. But handling Scripture responsibly is different from handling any other text responsibly at least in part because of the theological construals of Scripture that we have been exploring, which do not transfer to the more general case of reading any written text. Loosen the grip of these theological construals and there will of course be many other kinds of hermeneutical plurality that creep in, but they may not be characterized in the same way as being responsible to the biblical text as Scripture.

4

Biblical Hermeneutics
and *Kerygmatic* Responsibility

Matthew R. Malcolm

Wₕₑₙ ᴡᴇ ᴄᴏᴍᴇ ᴛᴏ ᴛʜᴇ Bɪʙʟᴇ we are largely dealing with ancient texts that have portions or degrees of "openness."[1] In relation to
the New Testament in particular, narrative, deliberative and apocalyptic texts frequently involve some elements of open suggestivity,
alongside more closed elements.

Mᴜʟᴛɪᴘʟᴇ Dɪᴍᴇɴsɪᴏɴs ᴏꜰ Pᴏᴛᴇɴᴛɪᴀʟ Fᴜsɪᴏɴ

Responsible readings of such texts, to oversimplify, arise from open, respectful engagement between the horizon of the text and the horizon of
the reader. In using this terminology I am, of course, entering into a

---

[1]Anthony C. Thiselton comments, "Wittgenstein and more explicitly Waismann confirm, in
effect, the view of Fuchs, Heidegger and Gadamer, that creative language requires a flexibil-
ity of usage or meaning which cannot be provided by completely 'closed' concepts or completely 'closed' assertions. . . . Wittgenstein rightly assumes that there are virtually endless
degrees of variation between completely closed and completely open horizons of meaning."
Anthony C. Thiselton, "Parables, 'World' and Eventful Speech: 'The Parables as Language-
Event: Some Comments on Fuchs's Hermeneutics in the Light of Linguistic Philosophy,'"
in *Thiselton on Hermeneutics: Collected Works with New Essays* (Grand Rapids: Eerdmans,
2006), p. 438.

tradition of hermeneutical reflection indebted to Schleiermacher, Heidegger, Gadamer, Thiselton and others. My intention is not to defend this tradition but to reflect creatively on the interpretation of the Bible from the standpoint of this broad tradition of philosophical hermeneutics. In Stanley Porter's contribution to this volume, he suggests that hermeneutical engagement must involve synchronic and diachronic dimensions. I would affirm this, and indeed I want to begin by exploring the multidimensional nature of human understanding, using my own terminology.

My proposal is that a reading of a text that shows heightened sensitivity across *multiple dimensions* of potential fusion will be more responsibly productive than a reading that lacks such multidimensionality.

Four dimensions of potential fusion, each of which might be seen to have synchronic and diachronic significance, are:

- The peculiar *realm* of the text, and its perception from the world of the reader

- The formational *mission* of the text, and the receptivity of the reader to such a formational setting

- The historical *emergence* of the text in space, time and language; and the familiarity of the reader with these elements

- The multifaceted mediating *reception* of the text that stretches across history to meet the reader

Each dimension will affect the others, and each may be brought into dialogue with the others to gauge the extent to which a particular reading involves harmony or dissonance.[2] Importantly for the present topic, then, each dimension of fusion represents a type of constraint on the proliferation of multiple valid interpretations. An interpretation at odds with the original language of the text as it emerged in history, for example, may rightly raise suspicion. Similarly, one might rightly be ini-

---

[2]Here I am struck by a parallel with Richard Briggs's commendation of bringing multiple construals into dialogue.

tially hesitant about a reading that defies the fruitful reception of the text since its emergence.

In engaging these dimensions of potential fusion, the responsible interpreter is essentially entering a hermeneutical circle by asking open, respectful questions of the text, from the perspective of the interpreter's own provisional, continually refining prejudices:[3]

Where is it coming come from? This relates to the *realm* of the text, which the reader provisionally posits or even inhabits. The answer might be: "the songs of the Beatles"; or "the late short stories of Anton Chekhov"; or "*The Guardian* newspaper"; or "early Christian literature"; or "the New Testament." There is no getting away from assuming some sort of provisional answer to the question of *realm* in order to approach a text. This realm may be made up of multiple worlds, each with their distinctive voices; nevertheless there is no need for such multiplicity to contradict the possibility of *some* sort of generality or concordance. Schleiermacher rightly notes that attention to the general is essential:

> Complete knowledge is always in this apparent circle, that each particular can only be understood via the general, of which it is a part, and vice versa. And every piece of knowledge is only scientific if it is formed in this way.[4]

In this volume, the contributions by Richard Briggs and Tom Greggs suggest one important answer to this question as it pertains to the Bible: the varied texts are all part of the one holy catholic apostolic Scripture, as affirmed by the ecumenical councils of the early church.

---

[3]Robert Morgan and John Barton rightly consider that "the more sophisticated theologians have always had their provisional theological frameworks prepared before doing their historical research. . . . Provided this prior understanding of the Bible is sufficiently flexible to be modified in the light of new evidence, it is appropriate to clarify it first." Robert Morgan with John Barton, *Biblical Interpretation*, Oxford Bible Series (Oxford: Oxford University Press, 1988), pp. 184-85.

[4]Friedrich Schleiermacher, "Hermeneutics and Criticism," in *Hermeneutics and Criticism and Other Writings*, Cambridge Texts in the History of Philosophy, trans. Andrew Bowie (Cambridge: Cambridge University Press, 1998), p. 24. Cf. p. 27, where Schleiermacher offers as a methodological rule the need to begin with a "general overview."

Why does it exist? What project does it contribute to? This relates to the *mission* of the text; its formational orientation. To make the question more concrete, one might ask, "To what broader mission does a Thiselton book on hermeneutics contribute?" or "What might be the broad project of Maurice Casey's work?" or "How might we characterize the larger enterprise of which Philipp Melanchthon was a part?" The more times around the hermeneutical circle, the better attuned this sense will become. One's perception of the mission of a text may sometimes be very broad, so much so that it may have never come to the conscious articulation of the author—or may grate with the conscious articulation of the author. Indeed, the formational *mission* to which a text might be said to belong is generally bigger than the immediate "purpose" or "occasion"; and attempting to perceive it may involve sensitive attention to external factors or subtle entextualization. The interpreter who is especially attuned to this dimension will be well equipped to push between the lines of the text, or carry on along the trajectory of the text, whether in sympathy or disagreement with the author.

How is it communicated? This relates to the *emergence* of the text in space, time, and language. This wide-ranging question has dominated the last two centuries of biblical interpretation, and in the early 1800s, Schleiermacher rightly noted that questions of genre, authorship, occasion and philology are indispensable:

> Everything in a given utterance which requires a more precise determination may only be determined from the language area which is common to the author and his original audience.[5]

Of course, engagement with a text that emerges from another space, time and language cannot be reflected upon with philosophical naivete. Hermeneutical inquiry demands some consideration of how language operates, and how it relates to reality and to thought.[6]

What are its impacts? This question relates to the *reception* of the text

---

[5]Schleiermacher, "Hermeneutics and Criticism," p. 30.
[6]As important as these issues are, they are not the topic of the current chapter.

in its post-history. Generations of interpreters develop reading traditions, bequeathing their findings and questions to subsequent generations. Some of these traditions will become stable over time, while others will be time-bound. The present-day interpreter will find their own assumptions and questions shaped, altered and resisted by such traditions. Indeed, the first point of contact between the present-day interpreter and an ancient text is not generally the text itself, in a pristine, uninterpreted vacuum, but rather the text as mediated, for good and for ill, by intervening generations.[7] The interpreter will need to perceive where such concretized readings have been fruitful, suggestive or abusive.

I consider these dimensions to be of general hermeneutical interest—not just for biblical interpreters. In their application to the New Testament, different eras have emphasized and excelled at different dimensions of potential fusion. The patristics assumed a concordant *realm* for the New Testament, a realm in which God speaks about his Son to his people through the canonical corpus. The dialectical theologians were highly attuned to a formational *mission* of the New Testament, in which humans were confronted and addressed with the *kerygma* about Christ. The historical critics were experts on the historical *emergence* of the New Testament texts, considering carefully their sources, forms, backgrounds and devices. The medieval interpreters were particularly aware of the mediating *reception* of the New Testament texts by the early church (although their critical faculties were employed subtly).

Priming in each of these areas will be of benefit to the responsible interpreter, without requiring a singular method of interpretation. Indeed, while Joel Green wishes to speak about a model reader of the

---

[7]Gadamer elucidates: "Time is no longer primarily a gulf to be bridged, because it separates, but it is actually the supportive ground of process in which the present is rooted. Hence temporal distance is not something that must be overcome. . . . In fact the important thing is to recognize the distance in time as a positive and productive possibility of understanding. It is not a yawning abyss, but is filled with the continuity of customs and traditions, in the light of which all that is handed down presents itself to us." Hans-Georg Gadamer, *Truth and Method*, 2nd rev. ed., trans. Joel Weinsheimer and Donald G. Marshall (London: Continuum, 2004) (translation of *Wahrheit und Methode: Grundzüge einer philosophischen Hermeneutik*, 2nd ed. [Tubingen: J. C. B. Mohr, 1960], pp. 264-65).

Bible, and Stephen Fowl and Richard Briggs urge the concept of a vir-
tuous reader of the Bible, I suggest that a concept that might be ruth-
lessly tied to general hermeneutics is that of a *primed* reader.[8] A primed
reader of the New Testament, whether Christian or secular, will be one
who is provisionally aware of a plurivocal realm; attentive to formational mission; competent with the emergent language, words, and
backgrounds; and critically engaged with the history of fruitful and
abusive reception.

Very often discussion of interpretation of the New Testament priori-
tizes the *emergent* dimension of the language, words and backgrounds.
Recently the dimension of *reception* has found heightened interest. In
this paper I want to focus on the dimension of the larger program of the
text—its formational orientation within a broad *mission*. That mission,
I suggest, has to do with apostolic *kerygma* or *kerygmata*.

KERYGMATIC MISSION

As James Dunn reminds us, the varied New Testament documents do
not speak their *kerygmata* in unison. Dunn sees that abstraction is inevitable if one attempts to discern a "core *kerygma*." He proposes that
the crucified and risen Jesus himself is the center and circumference of
Christian orthodoxy, but that his significance was expressed in a variety
of early kerygmatic formulations.[9]

In C. H. Dodd's classic treatment of the subject, he optimistically
attempts to discern an overarching unity of kerygmatic proclamation
but concedes at one point (at least) a plurality of voices, noting that the
Pauline kerygma is:

what he calls "my Gospel," and not necessarily the Gospel common

---

[8]I do not mean to belittle the usefulness of these other descriptions. Similar to my concept of
a "primed" reader is Green's concept of a "competent" or "practiced" reader: Joel B. Green,
"The Challenge of Hearing the New Testament," in Joel B. Green, ed., *Hearing the New
Testament: Strategies for Interpretation*, 2nd ed. (Grand Rapids: Eerdmans, 2010), p. 8.

[9]See James D. G. Dunn, *Unity and Diversity in the New Testament*, 3rd ed. (London: SCM,
2006), especially pp. 11-35.

to all or most early preachers. For Paul, as we know, claimed a high degree of originality in his presentation of the Gospel, and the claim is clearly justified.[10]

But while it may be inappropriate to describe early Christianity as speaking in monophonic unison,[11] that need not, of course, lead us to the conclusion that it speaks in polyphonic chaos. It may be justifiable to use the image of "symphonic concordance." In isolation, the offbeats of the snare and the melody of the oboe may sound unrelated or even jarring, but when they are taken as parts of a whole, they find superb coherence. But I would suggest that the post-Easter apostolic *kerygmata* are more closely related than snare and oboe. Paul appears pragmatically to expect a discernible apostolic coherence when he urges, "whether then it was I or they, so *we* proclaim, and so you have come to believe" (1 Cor 15:11). I think, then, that even while eschewing the general oversimplification and the overreliance on the book of Acts found in Dodd, Seeberg and others,[12] there remains a place for considering a somewhat coherent post-Easter kerygmatic mission in association with the New Testament documents, while conceding that *kerygma* may easily be broken up into *kerygmata*.

   Kerygmatic mission: Old Testament texts. Intriguingly, Dodd himself suggests that a singular source for such kerygmatic concordance may have been the historical Jesus' own utilization of Psalm 110. He comments:

> Wherever we read of Christ being at the right hand of God, or of hostile powers being subjected to Him, the ultimate reference is to this passage. In view of the place which Ps. cx.I holds in the New Testament, we may safely put it down as one of the fundamental

---

[10]C. H. Dodd, *The Apostolic Preaching and Its Developments: Three Lectures with an Appendix on Eschatology and History* (London: Hodder & Stoughton, 1936), p. 9.

[11]Brevard S. Childs concludes, "In sum, neither the abstraction of one unified kerygma according to Dodd, nor the projection of radical discontinuity within the tradition according to Bultmann has been sustained." Brevard S. Childs, *Biblical Theology of the Old and New Testaments: Theological Reflection on the Christian Bible* (Minneapolis: Fortress, 1993), p. 221.

[12]See the critiques surveyed in Benjamin Edsall, "Kerygma, Catechesis, and Other Things We Used to Find: Twentieth-Century Research on Early Christian Teaching Since Alfred Seeberg (1903)," *Currents in Biblical Research* 10/3 (2012): pp. 410-41.

texts of the primitive *kerygma*. Indeed, I can see no adequate reason for rejecting the statement of Mark that it was first cited by Jesus Himself in His public teaching in the Temple.[13]

This thought should not be downplayed on account of the subsequent overconfident attempts by Dodd, Lindars, Dahl and others to discern a precise historical sequence of developing christological interpretation in the early churches. It remains beyond question that a core group of Old Testament texts, headed by Psalm 110, is repeatedly seen as expressing the gospel about Jesus in the New Testament.[14]

Psalm 110 itself is used in at least Matthew, Mark, Luke, Acts, 1 Corinthians, Ephesians, Colossians, Hebrews and 1 Peter. We have no space to go through these, but I want to simply mention three places in which the first verse of this psalm is combined with Psalm 8: 1 Corinthians 15; Ephesians 1; and Hebrews 1–2 . In each of these places, the combined citations are taken up to express the exalted (yet God-subjected) authority of the died and risen human Messiah.

Kerygmatic mission: Traditional summaries. And regardless of the historical sequence of development, this sounds very much like the sort of message that is presented as a "passed-on" summary elsewhere in the New Testament.

In 1 Thessalonians 1:9-10, we hear the Pauline account of a *Macedonian tradition*:

> For they announce . . . how you turned to God from idols, to serve the living and true God, and to wait for his Son from heaven, whom he raised from the dead, Jesus, the one who rescues us from the coming wrath.

In Philippians 2:6-11, we encounter a *hymnic tradition*, in which Jesus is said to have descended to death, before being exalted by God to the

---

[13]Dodd, *Apostolic Preaching*, p. 24.

[14]As Brevard Childs rightly perceives, "the central role of the Old Testament in the church's understanding and interpreting the death and resurrection of Christ is incontestable." Childs, *Biblical Theology*, p. 229.

highest position, under which all things but God will be subject. In Acts 7:54, Luke recalls the death of Jesus in his account of the death of Stephen, while concurrently bearing witness to the rest of the familiar kerygmatic summary by putting on Stephen's lips a *scriptural tradition*:

He saw the glory of God, and Jesus standing at the right hand of God, and he said, "Look! I see heaven opened, and the Son of Man standing at the right hand of God."

In Revelation 5:12, we hear angels echoing what was presumably an Asian *liturgical tradition*:

Worthy is the slaughtered lamb to receive power and wealth and wisdom and strength and honor and glory and blessing.

Here we have no unified creed; but we do have a concordant symphony of traditional *kerygmata*, variously expressing grateful dependence on a died and risen Messiah who, while exalted, is subject to God, who remains on the throne.[15]

Kerygmatic mission: Liturgical activities. But a somewhat coherent apostolic mission is not just hinted by traditional summaries that appear in various New Testament documents; it is also suggested by a degree of similarity in liturgical activities attested in certain documents. In epistles such as Romans (Rom 6:3-4), 1 Corinthians (1 Cor 12:13), Galatians (Gal 3:27), Colossians (Col 2:12), and 1 Peter (1 Pet 3:21), the liturgical activity of baptism is associated with identity with the body of Christ, in death and/or resurrection. In each of the Gospels (Mt 26:26-27; Mk 14:22-23; Lk 22:19-20; Jn 6:51), as well as 1 Corinthians (1 Cor 10:16; 11:26), the liturgical sharing of the bread and the cup is associated with identity with the body of the Christ who was to undergo death and a future coming. These kerygmatic activities hint, albeit in a

---

[15]It might be suggested that such a summary represents the sort of abstract reduction against which Dunn warns above. I rather think of it as a synechdocal motif, which, while partial, evokes the broader symphony. In a similar way, the opening motif of Beethoven's fifth symphony is enough to evoke the whole, despite being insufficient as an encapsulation.

limited way, at a shared mission-setting associated with certain New
Testament documents.

Kerygmatic mission: Literary production. A broader hint comes from
the common production of new literary subgenres, in the four accounts
of the *Gospel* of Jesus Christ,[16] and in the discipling *Epistles* gathered and
shared between early churches before the end of the first century.[17] Not
only are these two new subgenres striking in their commonality of
purpose and content, they also bear surprising resemblances in micro-
construction and macroarrangement. With Professor Thiselton's encouraging supervision, I suggested in my doctoral dissertation[18] that the arrangement of 1 Corinthians is itself governed by Paul's *kerygma* of the
death and resurrection of the Messiah. And I suggest in my contribution
to his festschrift that a similar kerygmatic influence may be perceived, in
a variety of ways, in the arrangement of other New Testament epistles.

While 1 Corinthians moves from the cross, through its application to
ethics, to the resurrection, Ephesians and 1 Peter both move from the
renewing enablement granted by the Father through the resurrection of
the Messiah to an explication of Christian ethics. Philippians, on the
other hand, brings forth exemplar after exemplar of a kerygmatic orientation: deathly humiliation and awaited exaltation. There is no uniformity of approach here, and importantly, no uniformity of underlying *form*;[19] but there is a broad coherence of formational strategy.

---

[16]Richard A. Burridge argues that "the canonical gospels form a subgenre of βίοι Ἰησοῦ . . .
which displays a clear generic development from its origins in the oral traditions through
the primary stage of Mark to the classical secondary versions of Matthew and Luke. John
displays some minor variations on the theme." Richard A. Burridge, *What Are the Gospels?
A Comparison with Graeco-Roman Biography*, 2nd ed. (Grand Rapids: Eerdmans, 2004),
p. 243.

[17]Duane F. Watson comments on Paul's "modification of existing genres, which resulted in
the creation of a new genre. Paul is an apostle of a new gospel, an apostle who uses epistles
to praise, guide, and correct his churches." Duane F. Watson, "The Three Species of Rhetoric and the Study of the Pauline Epistles," in *Paul and Rhetoric*, ed. J. Paul Sampley and
Peter Lampe (New York: T & T Clark, 2010), p. 44.

[18]Matthew R. Malcolm, *Paul and the Rhetoric of Reversal: The Impact of Paul's Gospel on His
Macro-Rhetoric*, Society for New Testament Studies Monograph Series 155 (Cambridge:
Cambridge University Press, 2013).

[19]At this point I distance myself crucially from the early twentieth-century form critics.

And note that I am not making any claim about apostolic authorship; I am simply pointing to a cohering impetus given by the symphonic apostolic *kerygmata*.

THE PRIMED INTERPRETER

If we had more time, we could look beyond entextualized hints to external evidence of broadly coherent apostolic mission. Nevertheless, we have *primed* ourselves with a provisional sense of a broad kerygmatic formational mission: bearing witness to a core group of Old Testament texts, a variegated but concordant proclamation about the suffering and exalted Messiah, a variously attested experience of liturgical participation in this Messiah's body, and a common strategy in the production of new literary subgenres, numerous New Testament texts betray a formational program arising from apostolic post-Easter *kerygmata*. The primed reader will be appropriately attentive to this when interpreting the New Testament texts.

Just as we begin an Anton Chekhov story, or a Maurice Casey book, or an Anthony Thiselton essay with some image of the formational mission from which we sense it arises, and yet we are ready to have that sense surprised or refined, so we may approach the New Testament. The more conscious we are of our assumptions about formational mission, the more ready we will be to have these assumptions tested and cultivated. And the more ready we will be to ask creative but responsible questions of our texts.

Let me give an example. A primed reader will know that Paul's *kerygma* focuses on the humiliating death and vindicating exaltation of God's Messiah. This reader will know that Paul is not afraid to confront his hearers with the depths of the humiliation or the heights of the exaltation. In 1 Corinthians, Paul goes so far as to rub Christ's humiliation in the boastful Corinthians' faces, insisting that the God of the cross is powerfully weak (1 Cor 1:25); that the God of the cross chooses the weak (1 Cor 1:27); that the God of the cross has appointed weak apostles (1 Cor 2:3; 4:10); and that the God of the cross calls his people to imitate such weakness (1 Cor 4:16). So when this *kerygma*-primed reader reaches 1 Corinthians 8, they may be struck that this key word *weak* is used no less than five times of the one who abstains from idol meat: "their conscience is weak" (1 Cor 8:7); "to the weak" (1 Cor 8:9); "with a weak conscience" (1 Cor 8:10); "this weak brother or sister" (1 Cor 8:11); "their weak conscience" (1 Cor 8:12). And in the passage it is *only* this weak believer whose identity is explicitly bound to that of Christ: "this weak brother or sister for whom Christ died" (1 Cor 8:11); "When you sin against them . . . you sin against Christ" (1 Cor 8:12). On the other hand, no such assurance is given for the supposedly strong, who possess knowledge. It would be a responsible act of creativity for our primed reader to ask, "Just who is Paul really siding with in this passage—the strong or the weak?" Simply raising the question does not provide an answer, but a priming in a provisional sense of Paul's particular kerygmatic mission at least raises the question.

Another example: our primed New Testament reader, acquainted with the kerygmatic movement of 1 Corinthians from the denunciation of boastful rulers in favor of the cross (1 Cor 1–4), through to the abolition of such rulers at the time of future resurrection (1 Cor 15), may read the letter of James and ask: Why does *this* discipling letter likewise move from the denunciation of the boastful rich in favor of the lowly (Jas 1), through to the abolition of the boastful rich at the time of "the coming of the Lord" (Jas 5)? Again, simply raising the question does not provide an answer; but a priming in a provisional sense of concordant New Testament kerygmatic mission at least makes the question possible.

THE FAITHFUL INTERPRETER

But while being primed with a provisional sense of mission ought to result in responsibly creative questions from secular and Christian readers, it could be further asked: What sort of interpreter might be envisaged by the New Testament itself as most open and sensitive to this kerygmatic dimension of potential fusion? I suggest: a cruciform interpreter. One who is shaped by the cross is particularly attuned and open to the formational orientation of the *kerygma*, whether explicit or subtle.

We see this illustrated in Mark's Gospel, where James and John are shown to be unable to understand Jesus and his kingdom. Jesus says to them:

> You do not know what you are asking. Are you able to drink the cup that I drink, or be baptized with the baptism that I am baptized with? (Mark 10:38)

Then, in contrast to these cruciphobic, glory-thirsty disciples, Mark immediately presents us with an ideal disciple who can truly *understand*: the blind beggar, Bartimaeus. He understands who Jesus is, and he understands that a true disciple will cast off the past and follow Jesus to the place of his execution.

Jesus seeks interpreters such as these. And a cruciform interpreter, when you think about it, is a dead interpreter. It is at this point that the general hermeneutics we crave and affirm[20] has to descend to the tomb. But it descends to the tomb not to be extinguished as worthless, but to be resurrected as unapologetically Christian interpretation. *Christian interpretation, then, has continuity with, and arises from, general hermeneutics;*[21] but here the reader transcends from being *primed* in

---

[20]I am sympathetic to Petr Pokorný's insistence that "the interpretation of the Bible is not a hermeneutical operation for which fundamentally different rules of interpretation apply than for other texts." Petr Pokorný, *Hermeneutics as a Theory of Understanding*, trans. Anna Bryson-Gustová (Grand Rapids: Eerdmans, 2011), p. 8.

[21]My suggestion is that Christian *interpretation* is a "resurrected" embodiment of general *hermeneutics*. It neither pretends to exist unremarkably within general hermeneutics nor situates itself apart from general hermeneutics. I propose this as an answer to Stephen Fowl's concerns: "If one's interpretive practice is governed by a general hermeneutical theory (of any type), then it is very hard to avoid the situation where theological interpretation of Scripture becomes the activity of applying theological concerns to interpretation done on other grounds. It seems all too easy to allow a general theory of textual meaning to provide the *telos* of theological interpretation." Stephen E. Fowl, *Theological Interpretation of Scripture: A Short Introduction* (Milton Keynes, UK: Paternoster, 2009), p. 39. According to my proposal, Christian interpretation figuratively *arises* from general hermeneutics. The imagery of death and resurrection, with its connotations of continuity and discontinuity, is quite crucial here. It ought to be pointed out, furthermore, that the "death" is entered into voluntarily by the interpreter, in humble acknowledgement that human understanding is limited, provisional and ultimately dependent on the God who brings life from death. I am grateful to those who helped me "flesh out" this imagery after the conference presentation of this chapter in June 2012.

relation to the mission of the text to being *faithful* in relation to the mission of the text (together with their brothers and sisters). Furthermore, here, *kerygma* is no longer just to be acknowledged as a discernible formational orientation of New Testament texts; here, with Christian interpretation, it can be applied retrospectively to Old Testament texts as well, as the divine formational orientation that never made it to the conscious articulation of the human authors.[22]

Indeed, it is *only* here, with the faithful prejudice of Christian interpretation, that we are finally positioned to hear "all that the prophets have declared." What have they declared? According to 1 Peter, they "prophesied of the grace that was to be yours," hearing the Spirit of Christ who "testified beforehand to Christ's sufferings and his subsequent glory" (1 Pet 1:11). According to Paul, they wrote in accordance with the tenets that "Christ died for sins . . . was buried . . . was raised . . . appeared" (1 Cor 15:3-5). According to John, Isaiah "saw Jesus' glory, and spoke about him" (Jn 12:41). And as the Lukan Jesus himself says, "How foolish and slow-hearted you are to believe all that the prophets have declared. Was it not necessary for the Messiah to suffer these things and then enter his glory?" (Lk 24:25-26).

Here we see in practice creative biblical interpretation constrained by kerygmatic responsibility.

---

[22]Stephen Fowl cautions that expecting to find Christ "hidden beneath the surface of the OT" may result in an unhelpful pursuit of textual "excavation." I think that this problem can be avoided by rather configuring the pursuit as "informed trajectorization." Fowl, *Theological Interpretation*, p. 33.

5

Biblical Hermeneutics
and *Historical* Responsibility

James D. G. Dunn

LET ME BEGIN BY CLARIFYING what I mean or understand by "historical responsibility." As a term in this context, *historical* has a potentially wide referential sweep. Historians and readers of historical texts have become increasingly aware through the last century that they must be alert to their own history as they scrutinize the historical data or read the historical text. That awareness is of exceeding importance, since, not least, it reminds us that the hermeneutical circle is three dimensional. Equally important is awareness of the historical processes by which the data or the text has come to us, including the way in which the data or the text has been read. As Hans-Georg Gadamer, in particular, brought home to us, the interpreter and the act of interpretation are themselves caught up in the flow of history; both text and interpreter are part of a historical continuum, *Wirkungsgeschichte*.[1]

I regard all this as integral to responsible hermeneutics. In this in-

---

[1]H.-G. Gadamer, *Truth and Method* (New York: Crossroad, 1989), particularly pp. 282, 295-307. See further A. C. Thiselton, *The Two Horizons* (Exeter, UK: Paternoster, 1980), pp. 306-8; also *Thiselton on Hermeneutics* (Aldershot, UK: Ashgate, 2006), pp. 291-93.

stance, however, I focus primarily on the historical context from which the biblical text came, the historical context of the text's composition and original reception. That focus, in fact, becomes very blurred with most of the biblical writings. In the case of most Old Testament writings it is scarcely possible to ascertain an "original" author or "original" recipients. The documents that are present to us are certainly historically ancient, but in so many cases are the product of a lengthy process of oral tradition, composition, editing, recomposition, etc., with many authorial hands involved and diverse historical contexts in play, so that "historical" exegesis may have to include an attempt to trace the history of the tradition, even when the chief interest is on the final or canonical version of the text.

With most of the New Testament writings, however, enquiry into the historical context of an original writing is both plausible and possible. The undisputed Pauline letters are the product of a single author, whose intention in writing or dictating the letters is mostly as clear as could be hoped for in a historical document of its period. In most cases the letters were written or dictated in a set of circumstances and address recipients in a set of circumstances that can be fairly readily deduced from the letters themselves. Even if some of the letters are judged to be compilations of several letters (2 Corinthians and Philippians), the several letters are almost always attributed to Paul himself, though their historical contexts are inevitably more obscure. Most of the letters usually judged to be pseudepigraphal (including other members of the Pauline corpus), or whose author is unknown (notably Hebrews), can be dated within a ten- or twenty-year time span; and attribution of authorship (to Paul, or James, or Peter) can still tell us a good deal about the historical contexts of the letters. The Gospels create different problems, but consensus dating is again within a limited time frame, and in any case they reveal so much about the way Jesus was remembered in the two generations following his crucifixion and resurrection.

So, what can be usefully said about historical responsibility in the exegesis and interpretation of the New Testament writings—historical responsibility in the sense of setting the writings in the historical context of their composition and their purpose in being written? There are some basic principles that are all too obvious, but easily neglected and still needing to be asserted.

HISTORICAL LANGUAGE AS HISTORICAL LANGUAGE

Modernists and postmodernists should never forget, even for an instant, that the original languages of the Bible are ancient Hebrew (Aramaic) and Greek. To read the New Testament as a historical text, one must recognize its language as ancient Greek and read its words as such. If these words are to convey meaning they must be read within the context of the language usage of the time. To make sense of these ancient Greek words, we must know how these words functioned, what meaning they conveyed at the time the New Testament documents were written, what sense they would have conveyed to those for whom the documents were written. Historical philology is still essential and unavoidable. We today stand on the shoulders of the scholars of the Renaissance and the Reformation for their research into the meaning and usage of the Greek of the New Testament, a research still ongoing, encapsulated for us particularly by the Bauer *Wörterbuch,* in its successive editions.[2] Moreover, we have recognized afresh in the twentieth century that words are not constant units of meaning, but function within idioms, phrases and sentences, which shape the meaning of the words which they contain.[3] And with the steadily increasing knowledge of how the language of the New Testament functioned in everyday life (through papyri and inscriptions),[4] as well as in classical literature, we have a much clearer grasp of the range of usage of New Testament Greek and of the meaning it would have conveyed.

---

[2]W. Bauer, *A Greek-English Lexicon of the New Testament and Other Early Christian Literature,* 3rd ed., rev. by F. W. Danker (Chicago: University of Chicago Press, 2000).

[3]Particularly J. Barr, *The Semantics of Biblical Language* (Oxford: Oxford University Press, 1961).

[4]G. A. Deissmann, *Bible Studies* (English translation, Edinburgh: T & T Clark, 1901).

These points have been familiar for two centuries. Early in the nineteenth century Friedrich Schleiermacher defined the two canons of "grammatical interpretation" thus: "First canon. A more precise determination of any point in a given text must be decided on the basis of the use of language common to the author and his original public"; "Second canon. The meaning of each word of a passage must be determined by the context in which it serves."[5] And in the middle of the twentieth century Rudolf Bultmann made the same point in his essay "Is Exegesis Without Presuppositions Possible"[6]: "Every text speaks in the language of its time and of its historical setting. This the exegete must know; therefore, he must know the historical conditions of the language of the period out of which the text he is to interpret has arisen." It inevitably follows that the Greek text (even in its modern, eclectic form) is normative for any understanding of the text. That is the text that has to be understood. And it must first be understood as an ancient Greek text, as the ancient Greeks would most naturally have understood it.[7]

The basic point can be made with regard to *translation*. For, of course, the greatest circulation and use of the New Testament for centuries has been in translation. And translations have a life and influence of their own; they become the New Testament that is read and interpreted; one need only instance the King James Version whose fourth centenary we celebrated in 2011. But we must never forget that they are translations; their rights as texts are wholly dependent on the Greek texts of which they are translations. The point is that unless the Greek text is recognized as determining and limiting the range and diversity of translation,

---

[5]*Hermeneutics: The Handwritten Manuscripts by F. D. E. Schleiermacher*, ed. H. Kimmerle (English translation, Missoula, MT: Scholars, 1977); excerpted by K. Mueller-Vollmer, *The Hermeneutics Reader* (New York: Continuum, 1994), pp. 86, 90. See further A. C. Thiselton, *New Horizons in Hermeneutics* (London: HarperCollins, 1992), chap. 6.

[6]Rudolf Bultmann, "Is Exegesis Without Presuppositions Possible," *Existence and Faith* (English translation, London: Collins, 1964), p. 344.

[7]See further my discussion of "History, Hermeneutics and Faith," in *Jesus Remembered* (Grand Rapids: Eerdmans, 2003), sect. 6, on which I draw for this section.

then the translation loses its claim to legitimacy as a translation. Translators are not free to create their own text. There are such things as bad, or even (dare one say it?) *wrong* translations. Presumably postmodern teachers of ancient languages and texts do not dissent from this, and postmodern examiners of such translations mark them down like any other teacher. In the case of readings of the New Testament, the normativity of the Greek text implies that there can be bad readings, "bad" because they are based on poor translations. Put another way, it is simply important to recognize *the character of historical texts as historical texts.* For the Greek text read as an historical text (interpretations as well as translations taking account of accidence, syntax and idiom of the day) inevitably functions as a norm for legitimacy of modern readings too. Without that basic recognition, the particular text becomes no more than a lump of potter's clay, vulnerable to being shaped entirely by the whim of the interpreter (potter). In other words, the very identity of the text is at stake, and historical study and scholarly method are unavoidable if the New Testament and the Gospels are to be read at all.

To avoid unnecessary confusion, it should be stated explicitly that, of course, there is no such thing as a single correct translation of a foreign-language text, far less a perfect translation. Anyone who has had to engage in translation knows that there is no translation without interpretation, that interpretation is an inescapable part of translation. Individual words in both languages have ranges of meaning (polysemic, multivalent), and there is no word in one language whose range and cultural overtones exactly match those of a word in the other language. In translation, choices have to be made between words and idioms that are equally as close and equally as distant from the words and idioms of the original-language text. The abundant diversity of modern translations of the Bible is all the illustration needed. None of this, however, alters the point that the original-language text is what is to be translated/interpreted, and that each translation has to justify itself as a translation of that text. The historical text cannot determine the exact translation, but unless the text functions as some kind of norm for the translation, unless it is seen to provide a limiting factor on the diversity of acceptable translations, then translation itself becomes irresponsible. And what applies to language applies also to genre. It is not simply a matter of recognizing that poetry and prose function differently, that one should not read parable and allegory and metaphor literally. It is a matter of setting the New Testament writings within their historical contexts and recognizing how they would be read and were presumably intended to be read: "Gospel" as effectively a new genre, but probably to be filed under biography in the library of Alexandria; Acts as intended to be read as history, well within the range of ancient historiography, including novelistic traits and theological *Tendenzen*; pseudonymity as an accepted and quite proper way to honor a great teacher; apocalypse as a way breaking through to the higher reality that is claimed to lie behind the pressures and tensions of everyday life. To read the Revelation of John, for example, as anything approaching a straightforward prophecy of the future is simply to misread it. And to pick out elements of these diverse writings and weave them together in some schema, as in rapture and "left behind" teaching, is to abuse their distinctive characters. Historical responsibility means not treating them as all the same, a kind of lowest-common-denominator approach; it means rather respecting them in their distinctiveness, respecting their differences and diversity. Historical truth is too big, too diverse, to be squeezed into some ideological container or a set of univocal propositions. The inadequacy of the classic creeds and confessions in their attempts to squeeze that truth into fixed words and set formulae underlines the point. And when historical truth escapes from such constraints, the pastoral consequences can be both liberating and devastating.

LIVING TEXT IN LIVING CONTEXT

To abstract a historical text, like a New Testament writing, from its historical context is like lifting a goldfish from its bowl and expecting it to still function as a goldfish. Any suggestion that a historical text has a life of its own, and can be understood wholly or sufficiently in its own terms, from within itself, opens the door to *eisegesis* of all sorts. A New Testament text belongs to a family, and has family traits. Most New Testament texts consciously acknowledge dependence on what we call the Old Testament.[8] To recognize explicit (Old Testament) quotations is little problem, though what the New Testament usage tells us about the texts of the Hebrew Bible and LXX and how they were understood and used in the first century can be a fascinating exercise. But there are also New Testament passages that contain allusions to and echoes of Old Testament language, where Old Testament phrasing is used possibly without deliberate forethought, where the New Testament writer's language has been shaped perhaps unconsciously by familiarity with scriptural terminology. To recognize allusion and echo is to dip the toe into the stream of living tradition. To hear a lecture of a George Steiner is to become aware of and to some degree tuned into a vast harmony, a living tapestry of allusion and echo linking themes and images across centuries of literature.[9] To recognize Old Testament allusion and echo in a New Testament letter or a Gospel passage is to begin to sit with a first-century audience and to hear with their ears. The work of Richard Hays and Francis Watson[10] has made us much more alert to such allusions in Paul, to the interplay with Scripture in Paul's own theologizing, and thus has attuned our ears more to the echo-chambers of the first century.

The same is true in regard to the Jesus tradition. Nothing has been so debilitating of our efforts to enter imaginatively into the assemblies of the first Christians than the assumption that the spread, transmission and use of Jesus tradition can only be understood in literary terms, the copying and redaction of written sources. But if, as is virtually certain,

[8]The literature is immense; see, e.g., G. K. Beale and D. A. Carson, eds., *Commentary on the New Testament Use of the Old Testament* (Grand Rapids: Baker Academic, 2007).

[9]E.g., his lecture "Two Suppers," in his collected essays, *No Passion Spent* (London: Faber and Faber, 1996), pp. 390-419.

[10]R. B. Hays, *Echoes of Scripture in the Letters of Paul* (New Haven, CT: Yale University Press, 1989); F. Watson, *Paul and the Hermeneutics of Faith* (London: T & T Clark, 2004).

during the first generation of Christianity, the stories about and teachings of Jesus were circulating predominantly or almost exclusively in oral form, then we enter a very different world from our world of libraries, monographs and reference works. An inevitable corollary, of course, is that recognition of allusion and echo becomes much more challenging. But it is clear that oral Jesus tradition was known and influential well into the second century.[11] So if we are being historically realistic we simply cannot limit our recognition of the knowledge, use and influence of Jesus tradition to questions of a written Q and influence of written Gospels. And that loosening up of our conceptualization of how the Jesus tradition functioned, and how the Gospels came to be, has important consequences for our appreciation of the links between New Testament Gospels and letters and of how we should evaluate the tensions, divergences and discrepancies between the Gospels. Taking historical context seriously would have saved us from the worries about inconsistency and contradiction that have so plagued a too-literal reading of our sources and a too-literary understanding of the transmission process.[12]

It is a similar story with our tuning into the fuller religious context of first-century Christianity. Attempts keep being made to assert that the dominant sounding board was the wider Greco-Roman religious context—in particular, gnosticism, cynicism and the imperial cult. But *the* dominant sounding board was certainly Second Temple Judaism, both for Jesus and so also the Gospels, and for Paul. Here we have to acknowledge the long-term failure of New Testament scholarship to recognize the character of this relationship, the relationship between the New Testament texts, their authors and recipients, and the Judaism of the day. The attempt to define Christian identity, already in the second century, by distancing it from Judaism continued to distort our appreci-

---

[11]Special credit is due to H. Koester, *Synoptische Überlieferung bei den apostolischen Vätern* (Berlin: Akademie-Verlag, 1957).

[12]See, e.g., my "Reappreciating the Oral Jesus Tradition," *Svensk Exegetisk Årsbok* 74 (2009): 1-17.

ation of the historical context within which the New Testament writings should primarily be read through most of the twentieth century. Here above all the living context of the New Testament writings, as expressed through their allusions to, interactions with and reactions to the Judaism of the time, has had to be painfully reconstructed in the last sixty years. We should have learned far more than Christian scholarship did from the classic case of Martin Luther and his reading of Rom 1:16-17. As he himself relates,[13] what caused him his spiritual trauma was his reading of "the righteousness of God" as God's punitive judgment on sinners.

> For I hated that word "righteousness of God," which, according to the use and custom of all the teachers, I had been taught to understand philosophically regarding the formal or active righteousness, as they call it, with which God is righteous and punishes the unrighteous sinner.

But then he came to realize that "the righteousness of God is that by which the righteous lives by a gift of God, namely by faith." That is to say, he began to read Paul's phrase "the righteousness of God" within its Old Testament context, rather than as medieval philosophy had taught him. He realized that in Jewish covenant thought, God's righteousness was a saving rather than a punitive righteousness, as Romans 1:16-17 itself indicates: the righteousness of God as God's power to bring about salvation. As we now grasp more clearly, the Hebrew for "righteousness," *ṣĕdāqâ*, particularly in the Psalms and Isaiah, is often best translated as "salvation" or "vindication."[14] It was Luther's discovery of the historical context of this key theological phrase that launched the Reformation. Subsequent readings had become misreadings. The power of the scriptural word had been lost because it was not being read within its historical context.

The lesson that should have been learned then was quickly lost in the Lutheran setting of gospel and law in the sharpest antithesis. The con-

---

[13]*Luther's Works*, vol. 34 (Minneapolis: Fortress, 1960), pp. 336-37.
[14]See, e.g., contemporary translations of Psalm 51:14; 65:5; 71:15; Isaiah 46:13; 51:5-8; 62:1-2; Micah 6:5; 7:9.

viction that Judaism was narrowly legalistic, the caricature of Pharisees as killjoys and bigots, the working assumption that the authentic Jesus must have been different from and dissimilar to the Judaism of his day, continued to distort our understanding of the Gospels and appreciation of Jesus' mission well through the twentieth century. And still today most Jews and Christians regard Paul as the one through whom Christianity broke with Judaism, for Jew the great apostasy, for Christian the great liberation. It is only in the last generation that we have been able to question so many of these traditional taken-for-granteds. Discovery of the Dead Sea Scrolls, the publication only twenty years ago of the Halakhic letter from Qumran to the Jerusalem leadership justifying their separation from the rest of the people in terms of their understanding of "works of the law,"[15] the realization that Jews and Christians mingled freely in a kind of early ecumenism up until the fourth century, despite leaders' exhortations and warnings to the contrary[16]—such fuller appreciation of the historical context of writings such as Paul's letter to the Galatians, and the Gospels of Matthew and John, has made us much more sensitive to the living links between earliest Christianity and early Judaism within Christianity's canonical Scriptures which should determine our understanding of the Jewishness of Christianity and move Christian-Jewish dialogue on to a new plane, far more than has so far been the case. Reading the New Testament within its historical context liberates us from the bondage of ancient prejudices and safeguards us from falling into new ideological bondages.

In the same connection, nothing has been more important than the liberation of the New Testament from the lengthy tradition of Christian anti-Judaism and antisemitism. It is only when we approach the New Testament writings as first-century documents that we can make sense

---

[15]See my "4QMMT and Galatians," *New Testament Studies* 43 (1997): 147-53.

[16]I provide illustrations in "Two Covenants or One? The Interdependence of Jewish and Christian Identity," in *Geschichte - Tradition - Reflexion: Festschrift für Martin Hengel, III: Frühes Christentum*, ed. H. Lichtenberger (Tübingen: J. C. B. Mohr, 1996), pp. 97-122; repr. in *The Partings of the Ways* (London: SCM, 2006), pp. 339-65.

of what come across on first reading as anti-Jewish or antisemitic remarks and attitudes in the New Testament. A fundamentalist may well react negatively to a historical-critical approach to the text, but any unhistorical reading of the New Testament will find it hard to avoid an anti-Jewish reading of at least several New Testament passages—in particular, Matthew 27:25, the Jerusalem crowd shouting at Jesus' trial, "His blood be on us and our children," and John 8:44, Jesus' words to "the Jews," "You are from your father the devil." Such passages have provided the seedbed for centuries of Christian anti-Judaism, but so much of their potential to incite racial hatred can be weakened by setting them in their historical context. Within the context of intra-Jewish polemic and factional denunciations such passages lose their racial and anti-Jewish force.[17] Which is also why we should hesitate to allow such passages to be used in lection and liturgy without any reference to their historical context. We would scarcely allow the burnings of heretics and the drowning of alleged witches to guide present-day treatment of religious disagreement or social deviancy. So why should we allow instances of first-century vituperation to guide *our* attitude to the Jewish contemporaries of Jesus and the first Christians or to the Jews of today? Giving primacy to reading such texts in the historical context from within which they came and which shaped their character would save us from the literalness of the letter that kills.[18]

HISTORICAL TEXT IN SOCIAL SETTING

When we broaden out the issue of historical context to include social context we soon become aware of other historical dimensions of a New Testament text that are important for our understanding of the text and for the inferences that we may draw from the text. It is helpful to know, for example, that the great majority of Jesus' contemporaries would have

---

[17]L. T. Johnson, "The New Testament's Anti-Jewish Slander and the Conventions of Ancient Polemic," *JBL* 108 (1989): 419-41: "By the measure of contemporary Jewish polemic, the New Testament's slander against fellow Jews is remarkably mild" (p. 441).

[18]The allusion to 2 Corinthians 3:6 should be obvious.

been illiterate or at best semi-literate—probably less than 10 percent, a 10 percent made up almost entirely by scribes, social elite and officials. That historical fact would help inform our appreciation of the oral/literary debates already referred to. Again, to know that archaeology has demonstrated, for example, from the number of ritual baths, *miqwaôt*, discovered in Galilee as well as Judea, that ritual purity was a matter of high practical priority in the religious practices of Jesus' contemporaries, should help us evaluate more fairly Jesus' teaching on purity.

Similarly, when reading Paul's first letter to the Corinthians, it is not unimportant to know that homosexuality was quite common and highly regarded in Greek society. Also that casual sexual relations were quite acceptable—we recall, for example, the revealing comment of Demosthenes, "We have courtesans for pleasure, concubines for day to day care of the body, and wives to bear legitimate children."[19] Such information presumably makes the details of chapter 6 of 1 Corinthians much less eyebrow-raising than is likely to be the case otherwise. Equally it is important if Paul's teaching in chapters 8–10 of 1 Corinthians is to be more fully grasped for us to realize that the public restaurants of the day were part of temple complexes, where the meat served up would certainly be the excess meat from sacrifices to the temple's god (the bountiful availability of such meat was the reason why public dining rooms were so regularly attached to temples). Likewise, the regular translation of *exousia* as "freedom" or "liberty" in 1 Corinthians 8 and 9 misses the point that Paul was referring primarily to the *right* of Roman citizens to participate in civic banquets in such settings.[20] When these chapters are seen as a discussion of rights, rather than a more theoretical discussion of "freedom," their relevance both to the first-century context and to the twenty-first-century context becomes more apparent.

The failure to appreciate the historical context of the New Testament and its implications for our understanding of the New Testament has perhaps been nowhere more serious than in regard to *the role of women*

---

[19]Pseudo-Demosthenes, *Orations* 59.122.
[20]See my *Beginning from Jerusalem* (Grand Rapids: Eerdmans, 2009), pp. 802-10.

within the ministry of the church, particularly the issue whether women can be or should be ordained as priests or bishops. The most common appeal to the New Testament is to the fact that Jesus chose *only men* as his disciples, or apostles. In Roman Catholic tradition that argument, almost alone, is still regarded as sufficient to justify and give force to the subsequent tradition restricting ordination to men. There is no appeal to Jesus' own *teaching*. So far as we are aware, Jesus himself never spoke on the subject, never explained *why* he called only men to be his immediate disciples. The Gospels in fact attest that there were several women who played an important role among Jesus' close companions (Mk 15:41; Lk 8:1-3). But when it came to those whom Jesus was to send out on mission, two by two (Mk 6:7; Lk 10:1), one might well deduce that it was the most obvious policy for Jesus to use only men. How shameful it would have been to send out together a man and a woman who were not married! How shocking and dangerous to send out two women on their own! In other words, there are very good *social* and *cultural* reasons, social and cultural reasons much more relevant in first-century Palestine than in twenty-first-century Europe, why Jesus chose only twelve men to be his closest disciples. To assume that a *theological* reason, a theological assessment of the possible vocation and the ministerial potential of women, applicable in very different social and cultural contexts, is the *only* appropriate lesson to be drawn from Jesus' practice—that must be judged as at best tendentious and prejudicial, as *eis*egesis rather than *ex*egesis, reading *into* the text rather than *out from* the text.

But of course there are the passages in the Pauline letters which forbid women to speak in church (1 Cor 14:34-35), and forbid a woman to teach or have authority over a man (1 Tim 2:12)—or should that read, no *wife* should teach or have authority over her *husband*? (the Greek words, of course, having both meanings); here is an issue of interpretation that should not be ignored. Without ignoring these passages, however, we also need to take note of the passages in Paul that attest that of the coworkers of Paul's mission *twenty percent* were women. We need to note also that the first named Christian to be designated "deacon," as an ecclesiastical office, was Phoebe (Rom 16:1). It is very interesting to observe that until recently, translations translated the term as "deaconess" and translated the following term, *prostatis*, as "helper" (RSV). But we already knew that the Greek term, *prostatis*, means "benefactor" or "patron." So Phoebe was evidently not just the helper who made the tea after the worship service, but a very substantial figure and leader in the church in Cenchreae. Here what basic philology had already made clear was being blithely ignored by the unhistorical presumption that women could not have had such status in first-century Greece or the first-century church.

A few verses further down in Romans chapter 16, in his greetings to those in Rome, Paul refers to Andronicus and Junia, his kinsfolk, "who are outstanding among the apostles, who were also in Christ before me" (Rom 16:7). Here again older translations assumed that Paul must have been talking about two men—who else would have been described as "apostles"? So they translated Andronicus and *Junias*! But we now know that the male name Junias is nowhere documented in the Greco-Roman world, whereas the female name Junia is widely attested. That Paul was referring to a woman, Junia, was universally recognized by the commentators of the patristic period and beyond.[21] It must therefore be judged as the most obvious explanation that Junia (and very likely her husband Andronicus) were among the group that Paul elsewhere refers to as "all the apostles," to whom the risen Christ appeared before Paul's conversion (1 Cor 15:7). In the light of centuries of a male-dominated church one can understand why some have found it so difficult to accept women priests or even the thought of women bishops in the Church of England, not to mention the Roman Catholic Church. But to read Romans 16 as a first-century historical text tells us that the first acknowledged deacon was a woman, and that one of the outstanding apostles associated with the beginnings of the church of Rome was a woman. To

---

[21]E. J. Epp, *Junia, The First Woman Apostle* (Minneapolis: Fortress, 2005).

accept the meaning of such texts as they were evidently intended to be understood by Paul and presumably were understood by the recipients of his letter should have a higher priority, one would have thought, than the meaning imposed on them in conformity to church tradition.

"Historical responsibility," then, primarily means for me taking responsibility to read a New Testament text within the contexts in which and for which it was written, so far as that is possible. It means not allowing the assumption that it should only be read as it has been read within this or that church tradition to determine the meaning that we hear from it today. The incarnation of the Word within the historical context of first-century Palestine, if we take it seriously, inevitably means that the historical particularity of Jesus' mission and teaching must always be a determining factor in what we see Jesus, the incarnate Word, as revealing about God. Subsequent christological dogma that ignores the historical Jesus ignores the reality of the incarnation and abandons history for myth. So too with the inscripturated Word. A New Testament scripture divorced from its historical context is like a Christ divorced from the historical Jesus, a not after all truly incarnated Word. To ignore the New Testament's first-century context and meaning, to fail to keep meaning now heard closely related to the meaning intended by Gospel and letter writers, is to treat the New Testament as a hot-air balloon wafted by random winds and subject to the whims of whoever can bring it to earth.

6

Biblical Hermeneutics
and *Critical* Responsibility

Robert C. Morgan

A NUMBER OF THE CHAPTER TITLES in this collection confirm that its topic is not all biblical interpretation, but specifically Christian interpretation of Christian Scripture. However, Christians are part of a larger world in which some study the Bible without sharing the Christian presupposition that its essential subject matter is (or is related to) the revelation of God in Christ. The tension between religious and nonreligious biblical study has surfaced in different issues throughout the modern history of biblical scholarship, but since most biblical scholars have themselves been believers, the scale and shape of the problem have often[1] been underestimated. It was usually presented as an inner-Christian problem between liberals and conservatives. "Faith and criticism" was discussed by believers to persuade other believers that the new critical methods of studying the Gospels need not destroy their faith. Some sensed that a time bomb

---

[1]Before Karl Barth, one who sounded the alarm was Adolf Schlatter, e.g., in "Atheistic Methods in Theology" (1905), English translation in Werner Neuer, *Adolf Schlatter* (Grand Rapids: Baker, 1995), pp. 211-25.

was being laid at the doctrinal foundations of Christian faith, but unnecessary disputes about the Bible overshadowed the more urgent
christological questions.[2]

Nowadays competent Western interpreters from "any religion or
none" share methods that were largely pioneered by believers (on account of their stake in these texts) but do not presuppose religious belief.
That can be welcomed as making possible a conversation between believers and nonbelievers about the Bible. However, nonreligious
methods may foster nonreligious attitudes and perspectives. The bias
was offset and the danger neutralized by most students coming to serious biblical study as a result of their religious interests, but as biblical
scholarship has become more secularized, the issue has become more
visible. Most biblical interpretation has until recently been theological
interpretation, done by believers with religious aims and presuppositions. Where these are absent or can no longer be taken for granted
theologians need to be explicit about the character of their work and the
religious communities it serves. They may well admire nontheological
scholarship on the Bible, but its independence of religious presuppositions may reduce its religious value.

The use of secular methods in religious and theological reading of
Scripture is illuminated in Professor James Dunn's account of some as-
pects of biblical interpretation that are widely agreed on by Christian
and non-Christian readers of the Bible. The texts invite historical study,
and the methods that have been developed have proved fruitful. He
could have taken his assignment from a more theological angle and explained why history is so important specifically for Christians, but it was
reasonable for him to take both that and our cultural location for granted.
History is important for Christian faith, and we share well-tried methods,
and even some assumptions, with secular readers. Biblical scholarship
is open to all, but done in isolation from the issues discussed in the
earlier essays in this collection, the culture's nonreligious methods and

---

[2]Thus D. F. Strauss's 1835 *Life of Jesus* was attacked for what was largely right about its Gospel criticism rather than for its plainly intolerable christological proposal.

questions may deflect attention from the essential subject matter of Scripture. That concern stands behind the *Scripture and Hermeneutics* series[3] and may explain why those discussions said little about the theologian's *critical* responsibility. They owed much to Karl Barth's *Sachexegese* (theological exegesis) but disregarded Rudolf Bultmann's argument that *Sachkritik* (theological criticism) is a necessary aspect of that.[4] Bultmann's synthesis of theological interpretation and radical historical criticism was intensively discussed in the 1950s and '60s, but despite Professor Thiselton's pioneering work in *The Two Horizons* (1980) those hermeneutical debates had little impact on these English evangelical discussions.

Barth thought Bultmann's theological criticism of some scriptural texts in the light of the gospel they seek to articulate dangerously subjective, and there are legitimate concerns about interpreters having power over the biblical texts. Disagreement with some of what the Bible says suggests an attitude remote from the prayer that "we might hear, read, mark, learn and inwardly digest"[5] the holy Scriptures. Theological criticism needs self-critical reflection and dialogue with the text. But Scripture is to be read intelligently, and some forms of criticism are positive in both intent and outcomes. Textual criticism was soon accepted, despite its implications for belief in biblical inerrancy. Literary criticism also values and enjoys works of literature even when hijacked by cultural criticism. But historical criticism changes the focus from the texts themselves to their context or the history behind them, and the latter interest often involves a more negative critical attitude to the texts and its sources.

This turn to the history behind the texts, and neglect or reinterpretation of their religious truth claims, accounts for recent returns to a

---

[3]E.g., Craig Bartholomew, Colin Greene and Karl Möller, eds., *Renewing Biblical Interpretation*, Scripture and Hermeneutics vol. 1 (Grand Rapids: Zondervan, 2000).

[4]I have discussed this debate between Barth and Bultmann in "*Sachkritik* in Reception History," *Journal for the Study of the New Testament* 33, no. 2 (2010): 175-90.

[5]"Collect," Sunday closest to November 16, Year A, Book of Common Prayer (1979).

theological interpretation of Scripture that focuses on the texts themselves and their theological subject matter, and is not much concerned with some of the questions raised by historical critics. But the nontheological questions that arise in biblical study affect Christian faith and practice, and can create a perception that Christianity is discredited by modern historical research. It is possible to ignore the clash of religious and nonreligious approaches to the Bible, and concentrate on fostering the inner-Christian conversations with Scripture that are arguably our primary responsibility as biblical theologians, but the ambiguous relationship of faith and theology to the now-partly-defused historical-critical bombshell still requires attention.

One answer to the legitimate anxiety about the side effects of using secular methods in biblical interpretation is contained in this collection, beginning with several chapters concerned with other important dimensions of Christian scriptural interpretation. The question of secular methods was thus placed strictly within that larger context of religious practice and theology. That was once taken for granted in theological education, and it did not need to be made explicit and justified. As the presupposition of Christian faith weakened, English university biblical studies became more secular. German Old and New Testament theology, by contrast, remained embedded in church-related faculties of theology alongside dogmatics, ethics and practical theology. However different their methods, the religious presupposition remained in place.

Both *historical* responsibility and *critical* responsibility touch on the relationship between Christians' and non-Christians' interpretation of the Bible. All use the same methods, and share some of the same aims, but Christians presuppose the essential truth of the theological subject matter of the Bible, as others do not. Since our concern is only with Christian interpretation of Scripture, we can take for granted the literary and historical critical *methods* shared by all scholars and consider their use in a more controversial kind of criticism. "Theological criticism" of Scripture is contested, but those who are justifiably suspicious of it recognize that other Christians think that this also is part of their theological responsibility.

It would take more than a few pages to persuade anyone not already persuaded that some of the problems in Scripture call for a "theological criticism" that repudiates some biblical texts, let alone to unfold a proposal about how this can be done without damaging the indispensable witness of Scripture to the gospel. Nobody doubts there are some difficult texts, but the difficulties can sometimes be avoided by proposing a more or less plausible alternative meaning for them that accords with the gospel. That unacknowledged theological criticism of what some texts say became a central feature of Christian reading of the Old Testament in allegorical interpretation where the literal meaning was not denied but was where necessary subordinated to one more "worthy of God." However valuable in prayer and preaching, in theology this needed the control provided by the literal meaning of other parts of Scripture,[6] and perhaps a magisterium to say which interpretations uncontrolled by reason can be trusted.

Allegorical interpretation provides the clearest indication that theological interpretation of Scripture is not simply a matter of exegesis, clarifying what the texts say. It has always been a matter of saying what (for Christians) they mean, and this meaning is shaped by an ecclesial context in which their Christian theological subject matter is presupposed. How that subject matter is understood is itself dependent on Scripture, and the ecclesial context is *semper reformanda* in the light of Scripture. Protestants and Catholics have accorded different weight to tradition, and taken different attitudes to a magisterium, but there has always been some kind of dialectic between the letter of Scripture and believers' sense of what Christianity or the gospel essentially *is*. The relationship between them is required by Christianity's locating the revelation of God in the Christ witnessed to in Scripture, but identifying them is over-simple.

---

[6]As Thomas Aquinas insisted: *Summa Theologiae* I.1.9.

Allegorical interpretation enabled the church to retain the Old Testament as Scripture, but claiming that a text means something different from what it says lost credibility as modern philological and historical exegesis became more powerful, and these rational methods came to determine much Christian scriptural interpretation in the West. Even accepting its role in building up and expressing faith, allegorical interpretation is no longer a preferred instrument of theological criticism. Its place in performing that particular task has been taken by historical criticism, but this has tended to damage the witness of Scripture to the gospel by eroding confidence in its truth, and more fundamentally because it does not speak normatively of God. Our question is therefore how this rational and often rationalistic instrument can perform theological criticism, clarifying rather than annihilating the gospel message of God in Christ.

Paul's dialectic between Scripture and the gospel provides a possible model. Scripture is seen as indispensible witness to the gospel, but is not identified with it. This dialectic was first applied to the New Testament by Marcion, disastrously. It was also applied one-sidedly by Luther, and within that tradition by Bultmann and Käsemann, among others. The results were problematic, but it is possible to see where they discard too much, and to propose a more canonical form of it within a New Testament theology that stops well short of Luther's canon criticism, Bultmann's demythologizing and Käsemann's "canon within the canon." These proposals have their place in theological reflection on Scripture but cannot have the last word. Some parts of the New Testament are more important than other parts, but the canon itself is axiomatic for traditional Christian identity. It can be interrogated and even criticized in theology but not set aside there, as it must be in historical constructions of Christian origins. Any theological interpretation of the New Testament as a whole will make some statements central, some peripheral, and may explain a few as intelligible in their historical context, but not normative for contemporary Christianity, because they are at odds with the gospel they intend to proclaim. There is here some risk of massaging the gospel to suit our own preferences and reading these into the biblical texts, but this can be countered by self-criticism and by reactions from the wider community, and by a recognition that Scripture is sometimes our God-given "adversary" (Luther).

Combining traditional Christian belief, or at least its essentials, with the historical criticism of Scripture has been the task and achievement of New Testament theology over more than two hundred years. This discipline has sometimes made historical criticism a vehicle of theological reflection, both clarifying the Christian gospel and on occasion criticizing what some interpreters have thought (subject to correction) inadequate expressions of it.

The theological discipline properly called New Testament *theology* is now being squeezed from opposite sides by an aggressively secular biblical scholarship on the one hand, and an explicit theological interpretation of Scripture on the other. But this squeezed middle is the place where theological criticism of Scripture can take place without it destroying Scripture's necessary witness to the gospel. Old and New Testament theology are best understood as Christian theological interpretation of Scripture within the constraints of a modern biblical scholarship whose historical criticism does not speak normatively of God—at least, not explicitly. How its historical criticism can be a vehicle of theological criticism was explored by Bultmann (footnote 4 above) and will be illustrated from Christology and gospel criticism below. Our discussion will not include the Christian theological discipline called Old Testament theology, nor the possibility of combining the two disciplines in an overarching "biblical theology." What the New Testament presupposes of the Old belongs to the scriptural *norm* of Christian faith and theology and is ideally to be included in a New Testament theology[7] that interprets the twenty-seven texts that are most

---

[7]F. Hahn, *Theologie des Neuen Testaments*, Band II (Tübingen: Mohr Siebeck, 2002), pp. 38-142, discusses at length "the Old Testament as Bible of early Christianity," but constraints of space justify much of the relevant material being demitted to Old Testament theologies. These too are important because, as a source of Christian preaching, faith and

directly definitive of Christian identity. These may arguably be scruti-
nized critically when being interpreted theologically.

In contrast to Barth's speaking *with* Paul, and so himself speaking
normatively of God, two of the greatest admirers of Barth's 1922 commentary, Kingsley Barrett and Ernst Käsemann, wrote historical-
critical commentaries on Romans closer in form if not in content to
those that Barth had criticized. They explained Paul's thought (as they
understood it), but explained it descriptively rather than normatively,
even though their own personal sympathies and commitments were
no secret.[8] In other words, they were New Testament theologians.
Their commentaries (like Hoskyns and Bultmann on John) contain
some theological interpretation, but it is theology in and through
historical-critical exegesis. These New Testament theologians allowed
the normative theological dimension to remain *implicit*, in contrast to
Barth's *explicit* theological interpretation of Scripture. That was the
price they paid as Christian theologians for working within the limits
of historical critical reason, and they paid it because modern
scholarship yields some truth and the conversation with nonbelievers
is worth maintaining. It does not entail any sacrifice of the theologians'
own religious beliefs.

Discussion of this New Testament theological discipline working
with the historical-critical and exegetical methods shared with non-
theologians has usually said more about its methods (and the aims associated with these) than about its religious and theological aims. It has
therefore tended to slide into a purely historical project. Using secular
methods induces secular perspectives. This misunderstanding can again
be corrected, despite some recent resistance from both historians and
theologians, and a New Testament theology cultivated that mediates
between the religious discourse of explicit theological interpretation or

---

theology, the Old Testament requires responsible interpretation that takes seriously its
historical as well as its canonical contexts.
[8]See Barrett's preface to the first edition of *The Epistle to the Romans* (London: A & C Black,
1957), p. vi. Käsemann told me he read Barth's second edition five times as a student.

dogmatics on the one hand and a purely historical secular biblical scholarship on the other.

The alternative to a mediating New Testament theology is for those other two ways of reading the Bible to exist in parallel (as they do), independent of each other, the one addressed to the church, the other to a secular culture and academy. But any such a wedge between faith and the dominant rationality risks depriving theology of the truth discovered in critical biblical scholarship. Systematic theologians who advise biblical scholars to leave the theology to them must know that a vibrant theological study of the Bible has always been a necessity for the church. It is surely unwise to distrust biblical scholars who want to engage in that indirectly in implicit theological interpretation. These biblical scholars see themselves as historical *theologians* and exegetes, not merely historians of theology and grammarians. There is a difference between New Testament theology and preaching, but they are related, and this discipline (as well as explicit theological interpretation) can inform and sustain (rather than erode) Christian preaching and other religious reading of Scripture.

There are several reasons why an *explicit* theological interpretation is insufficient for the church, and why the *implicit* theological interpretation provided by a theological New Testament theology within the constraints of modern biblical scholarship is also necessary. One is that the latter can best deploy biblical scholarship to meet the critical responsibilities of theology. Speaking "with" Paul (or any other witness) leaves no scope for challenging anything they say, whereas describing and comparing this with the whole New Testament witness may help correct any one-sidedness. The integrity of the scriptural witness allows for questionable formulations at the margins.

This *critical* aspect of Christian interpreters' moral and theological responsibility has been met through historical criticism within Old and New Testament theology. Historical judgments can imply a theological challenge to the truth of a text. These disciplines use literary and historical-critical methods, but their primary aim is theological reflection on the biblical texts, not historical reconstruction of ancient religions. The criticism serves reflection on the gospel to which the texts bear witness, some more adequately and more powerfully than others. It makes room for a critical theological reflection that presupposes that the texts speak of God but cautiously allows for an element of evaluation.

That is what some Bible-believing Christians resist, preferring to limit themselves to an explicit theological interpretation informed by a historical research which knows its limits and does not become an instrument of theological criticism. The justification for this resistance is that theological criticism through historical criticism has often proved destructive and has reduced and obscured the gospel it seeks to clarify. Marcion is a clear example. His unwarranted historical hypothesis cut the gospel from its Jewish roots and the Christian God. Bultmann tried to limit his early *Sachkritik* to an immanent criticism of a few Pauline texts in the light of the gospel the author intended to proclaim,[9] but his radicalization of *Sachkritik* in his demythologizing proposal excluded dimensions of the text not amenable to his *existentiale Interpretation*. Käsemann's *Sachkritik* sharpened the point of the Pauline witness to Christ at the expense of other New Testament witnesses whose "early Catholicism" contradicted his Lutheran understanding of the gospel. But by far the most damaging example of theological criticism through historical criticism destroying the New Testament witness is the Enlightenment project of pitting the "historical Jesus" against the biblical witness to the crucified and risen Lord. Our proposal for historical criticism functioning as a vehicle of theological criticism without subverting the gospel must therefore be tested in this most sensitive area in New Testament theology where it impinges on how Christians think and speak of the crucified and risen Jesus.

Christian interpretation of the canonical Gospels and the rest of Scripture presupposes belief in God decisively revealed in Jesus. Clergy and others engage in explicit theological interpretation of Scripture when they preach in accord with its witness, typically speaking of God

---

[9]See Rudolf Bultmann, *Faith and Understanding* (London: SCM Press, 1969), pp. 66-94 (German 1926).

in Christ *with* a New Testament writer, and contemplating what might, with Martin Kähler, be called the "biblical Christ," taking that umbrella phrase to cover any number of possible "faith-images" of Jesus that are in accord with the biblical witness.[10] Preachers share with the congregation their Christian "faith-images" of Jesus. Some Christians also engage in historical Jesus research—not from the pulpit, but in classrooms and perhaps also in parish groups—and would think it odd to be told that this was either historically impossible or religiously and theologically irrelevant. Kähler's disapproval of the so-called historical Jesus of a David Strauss or a Joseph Renan was not a rejection of historical Jesus research as such.[11] Understanding why he rejected these and other historical portraits of Jesus will explain why many Christians have similar reservations about the historians' Jesuses produced by E. P. Sanders or J. D. Crossan, not to mention the so-called Jesus Seminar.[12] These contain more or less good historical research but seem not to be written from the perspective of resurrection faith. The Jesus books of Günther Bornkamm (1956), Anthony Harvey (1982), Gerd Theissen (1986 and 1996), Tom Wright (1996) and James Dunn (2003), on the other hand, are religiously more satisfying precisely because they are broadly New Testament theology, constructed from historical and exegetical research, but with religious and theological as well as historical interests and intent, sharing the essentials of the Evangelists' Christian (i.e., resurrection-faith) standpoints.

Some of the methods used in historical Jesus research have been challenged and refined,[13] and many conclusions have been modified or re-

---

[10]Martin Kähler, *The So-Called Historical Jesus and the Historic, Biblical Christ* (1892, 2nd ed. 1896; English translation, Philadelphia: Fortress, 1964). For his concept of *Bild*, translated here "faith-image," see especially pp. 77-88.

[11]Kähler shared their resistance to "an abstract dogmatism" but would reject any portrait that ignored or denied the truth of resurrection faith.

[12]L. T. Johnson, *The Real Jesus: The Misguided Quest for the Historical Jesus and the Truth of the Traditional Gospels* (New York: HarperCollins, 1996), adopts Kähler's stance in his critique of the California "Jesus Seminar."

[13]The criteria of authenticity have also been improved, e.g., N. T. Wright, *Jesus and the Victory of God* (London: SPCK, 1996), p. 132; G. Theissen and D. Winter, *The Quest for the Plausible Jesus* (Louisville: Westminster John Knox, 2002; German 1997).

jected. Most theologians and biblical scholars now agree with Kähler that the Gospel sources do not warrant the kind of modern biographical portraits that even scholars once attempted. The criticism of those older "lives of Jesus" by subsequent historical research provides a prime example of historical criticism functioning as an instrument of theological criticism, just as the liberal "lives" had themselves used historical criticism against dogmatic constructions that they thought untrue or inadequate. In each case, Christians were dissatisfied with older portraits on both religious and rational grounds, and they used rational historical-critical methods to discredit them, and (they hoped) to replace them with something more religiously and rationally satisfying.

Their rational aims were more successfully achieved than their religious ones. The minimal sketches that stand up to rational scrutiny still seem to many Christians religiously inadequate. Historical criticism has proved more powerful in tearing down than in building up, and many Christians have therefore held it at arm's length. Some of them have echoed Kähler's misleading title and preferred a "historic, biblical Christ" to a "so-called historical Jesus." But Kähler welcomed the historians' clarification of Jesus' genuine humanity and cannot have intended the sharp dualism that others read into the two terms of his title. That would be religiously and theologically fatal. Christians believe that their faith-images of Jesus are true. The historical element they contain must therefore be assumed to stand in some positive relation to the historical actuality. Not very much about Jesus is known for sure, and that leaves room for the contribution of historical imagination within Christians' faith-images, but they do have to be credible. They do not have to be demonstrable by historical research, but they can in principle be falsified by it. Theologians therefore encourage faith-images of Jesus that will stand up to historical scrutiny while going beyond what is historically verifiable. New Testament theology offers historically defensible portraits drawn by theologians who share the Evangelists' resurrection faith perspectives, however diversely that mystery is understood today.

The faith-images once constructed by harmonizing the four canonical portraits have proved problematic, however biblical. In practice many Christians allow more or less historical judgment into their readings of the Gospels in the process of constructing or developing and living with the mobile and plastic faith-images through which they know and relate to their Savior. The religious quest for a credible Jesus is seen to require historical Jesus research, though not complete historical reconstructions. The larger constructions of some historians tend to be religiously inadequate, partly because the evidence is fragmentary and faith-images require more than can be verified by historical research, but more importantly because historical reconstructions do not relate Jesus normatively to God. They can at best say he thought he was sent by God. Christian faith, on the other hand, says he *was* sent by God, however that is then elucidated. New Testament theologians restrict themselves to the historical statement, but imply their assent.

Christian interpretation of Scripture, based on traditional Christian faith, prefers its "biblical Christs" to most critical historical reconstructions, because the latter exclude (or minimize) questions of religious truth. So far, so Kähler—against Renan and Strauss. But Kähler's "biblical Christ" was not a mere harmony of the four Gospel portraits. His acceptance of historical Jesus research must have influenced his pietist faith-images of Jesus. These will have incorporated his own historical reflection and judgments. What mattered was that this historical Jesus research took place within the context of his Christian belief in the crucified and risen Jesus. Unlike "biblical Christs" that do not admit the few highly probable results of modern critical historical research, and unlike purely historical reconstructions of Jesus that discount Christian faith and experience of the risen Lord, his faith-images could include all the critical historical research that he considered reliable into a "biblical Christ" that was historically credible even though seen through the lens of his resurrection faith.

This presupposes the resurrection of Jesus but does not claim it is amenable to historical research. It is a category mistake to confuse a believed-in and confessed divine event in history with the data of modern critical historical research. The nineteenth-century concept of *Heilsgeschichte* (the story of our salvation) depended and foundered on that category mistake. Arguing for the reliability of some resurrection traditions admittedly has apologetic value.[14] Hermann Samuel Reimarus was wrong about some things. Discrediting the legends has been a way of denying the truth and eroding belief in the divine vindication of Jesus. But the resurrection of Jesus is confessed as the central mystery, not reduced to history, or seen as one miracle among others. It can be understood in various ways, and our language is necessarily metaphorical, but it is axiomatic for traditional Christianity and its talk of Jesus. It is not adequately represented as the last chapter or epilogue in books about Jesus but is the lens through which all the Jesus traditions are read by Christians before any provisional judgments are made about the historicity of one or another of these traditions. Apologetic considerations apart, it is best discussed in the first, introductory chapter of a Christian presentation of Jesus, not in the last.

All this confirms that the appropriate form of a Christian account of the history of Jesus is as part of a New Testament theology, in which resurrection faith is presupposed, but not used as evidence in argument, rather than historical reconstructions that reject that perspective and so implicitly deny the Christian claim. The 1950s and '60s Bultmannian theological "new quest of the historical Jesus" provides clear examples of this implicit theological interpretation of Scripture, notably Käsemann and Günther Bornkamm, found also in the Jesus books of Andrew Harvey, Gerd Theissen, Dunn and Wright. These also fulfil a Christian apologetic function as good history, engaging with non-Christian historical constructions and perspectives on Jesus. That precludes arguments based on the modern authors' own Christian presup-

---

[14]N. T. Wright, *The Resurrection of the Son of God* (London: SPCK, 2003), pursues this line of argument most thoroughly, revealing its strengths and limitations.

positions, but allows for plausible historical narratives compatible with resurrection faith.[15]

This account of the character and place of a critical historical Jesus research in Christian faith-images of Jesus illustrates at its most sensitive point the critical historical responsibility accepted in some Christian theological interpretation of Scripture. Other examples of theological criticism in and through historical criticism deserve attention.[16] Doing theological criticism through historical criticism in complete New Testament theologies reduces the risk of truncating the canon in favor of one's preferred biblical witnesses. These textbooks can offer implicit theological interpretations of Scripture as a whole, and of individual biblical books, topics or passages. Trying to speak adequately of God as known in Jesus gives priority to the theological interpretation of the four Gospels. Whether the critical historian's contribution should also empower New Testament theologians on occasion to question, say, an Evangelist's anti-Judaism, or the view of women betrayed by 1 Corinthians 11:3-9[17] or 1 Timothy 2, or Paul on homosexuality, or Matthew's predilection for hellfire, by arguing historically that they misrepresent Jesus' own position and ethically that they are morally repugnant, contributing to a cumulative theological case that they misrepresent the gospel, remains open to debate.

---

[15]I have rehearsed some objections to the ambiguous and often tendentious phrase "historical Jesus" in Jan G. van der Watt, ed., *The Quest for the Real Jesus* (Leiden: Brill, 2012).

[16]My essay on "Expansion and Criticism in the Christian Tradition," in M. Pye and R. Morgan, eds., *The Cardinal Meaning* (The Hague: Mouton, 1973), pp. 59-101, discusses a few.

[17]M. Lakey, *Image and Glory of God* (London: Continuum, 2010), offers a fine analysis of the hermeneutical issues in evangelical discussions of this "headship" text.

7

Biblical Hermeneutics
and *Relational* Responsibility

Tom Greggs

CONTEMPORARY ATTEMPTS AT BIBLICAL interpretation from within the magisterial Protestant traditions face a number of difficulties that arise from the traditions' affirmation of the Scripture Principle.[1] Although the tradition of *sola scriptura* claims that Scripture is sufficient and clear, biblical criticism surely points to the reality that Scripture is not univocal (if vocal at all) on many classical doctrinal loci (such as the hypostatic union or the doctrine of the Trinity); and biblical hermeneutics must surely remind contemporary Protestant readers of Scripture that they read through the lens of confessional documents, and certainly through the lens of the four principal ecumenical councils (and most especially through the lens of the Niceno-Constantinopolitan Creed and the Chalcedonian symbol). However, elements of the

---

[1]Wolfhart Pannenberg identifies difficulties in relation to hermeneutics *and* biblical criticism. This essay will deal only with the former of these two concerns. See Pannenberg, *Basic Questions in Theology, Volume 1* (Minneapolis: Fortress, 2008), pp. 1-14. An interesting (if somewhat basic) discussion of tradition in relation to canon, development and church history can be found in Emil Brunner, *The Misunderstanding of the Church* (Philadelphia: Westminster, 1951), chap. 4.

symbols and creeds do not clearly and straightforwardly say what Scripture seems to, about, for example, the relation of the Father to the Son.[2] On the one hand, this has led a number of evangelically minded Protestant systematic theologians to undertake a path well trodden by more radical Reformers in questioning the veracity of the creedal and symbolical reception in light of a more direct biblical engagement. Individual engagements with the biblical texts have been used to deny, for example, the eternal generation of the Son, effectively advocating some form of subordinationism.[3] One can understand how particular (modern, perhaps) understandings of *sola scriptura* might easily lead one to this conclusion. On the other hand, a number of people have recognized some of the tensions that exist in terms of the relation of the traditions of classical Christianity to the texts of Scripture, and have sought to explain this issue in a way which does not give hierarchical priority to Scripture in the way that *sola scriptura* classically has done. For example, in a recent book published by InterVarsity Press, Jim Belcher describes the approach of relational hermeneutics as follows:

---

[2]We see this, for example, in recent literature about Arius, in which he is presented as one who understands himself to be a biblicist. See, for example, Rowan Williams, *Arius: Heresy and Tradition* (London: SCM, 2001); and Robert C. Gregg and Dennis E. Groh, *Early Arianism: A View of Salvation* (Minneapolis: Augsburg, 1981). This perspective certainly seems appropriate to what primary sources there are, and even Athanasius resisted use of the nonbiblical term *homoousios* until ca. A.D. 355, preferring biblical terminology to point toward the same concept instead in his pre-355 works.

[3]See, for example, Bruce Ware, *Father, Son, and Holy Spirit: Relations, Roles, and Relevance* (Wheaton, IL: Crossway, 2006); idem, "How Shall We Think About the Trinity?" in Douglas S. Huffman and Eric L. Johnson, eds., *God Under Fire: Modern Scholarship Reinvents God* (Grand Rapids: Zondervan, 2002); Wayne Grudem, *Systematic Theology: An Introduction to Biblical Doctrine* (Downers Grove, IL: InterVaristy Press, 1994), pp. 248-52; idem, *Evangelical Feminism and Biblical Truth* (Sisters, OR: Multnomah, 2004); Stephen D. Kovach and Peter R. Schemm Jr., "A Defense of the Doctrine of the Eternal Subordination of the Son," *Journal of the Evangelical Theological Society* 42 (1999): 461-76. These claim that the creed is supportive of their position. However, also see the replies to this issue in defense of the classical doctrinal position, including: Kevin Giles, *The Eternal Generation of the Son: Maintaining Orthodoxy in Trinitarian Theology* (Downers Grove, IL: IVP Academic, 2012); idem, *Jesus and the Father: Modern Evangelicals Reinvent the Doctrine of the Trinity* (Grand Rapids: Zondervan, 2006); idem, *The Trinity and Subordinationism* (Downers Grove: IVP Academic, 2002); Thomas H. McCall, *Which Trinity? Whose Monotheism?* (Grand Rapids: Eerdmans, 2010), pp. 175-88.

"Nothing is privileged, not even the Bible, over the community in discovering and living out truth. The Bible is just one of the conversation partners."[4] This understanding of the issues relating to the relative authority of Scripture and church is a long way from *sola scriptura* as classically articulated in the Protestant tradition.

In this chapter, I will advocate that the activity of reading Scripture through the creeds and symbols of the first four councils is an exercise in reading Scripture with relational responsibility not only to the church of our own day, but to the communion of saints through all ages. When I speak of *relational responsibility* or *relational hermeneutics,* I am using the term to point toward the concrete reality that in the life of the church Scripture is not only read privately and understood individually, but it is first read publicly and understood corporately. The *church* (as individual believers united in the body of Christ) has always sought to understand Scripture, and it has been Scripture and its interpretation that has defined the church, as—in relation to one another and the text— the church has sought to understand the Word of God. This process of identification of the church around shared and relationally negotiated interpretation of Scripture is something we see in the church's path toward creedal and symbolic statements in the first five centuries. Furthermore, in setting a dense coda on Scripture, creeds and symbols offer minimal parameters within which Scripture continues to be interpreted for those who identify themselves as existing in relationship to the church in every age, through the communion of saints. Thus, for creedal Christians, the exercise of understanding Holy Scripture is always in one sense corporate, and an exercise that displays relational responsibility in interpretation, since the Christian does not exist except as part of the body of Christ.

By identifying the creeds and symbols as the church's exercise in reading texts relationally, in order to offer minimal parameters for responsible reading in the formation of doctrine for the community that

---

[4]Jim Belcher, *Deep Church: A Third Way Beyond Emerging and Traditional* (Downers Grove, IL: InterVarsity Press, 2009), p. 145.

identifies as the church, I will seek to demonstrate that creedal interpretation of the Bible does not stand at odds with classical Protestant accounts of *sola scriptura*. I will do this, first, through identifying the hierarchical priority of Jesus Christ over Scripture, and of Scripture over the church; second, by seeking to understand councils and symbols as arising from relational readings of the biblical canon, and as giving form to relational patterns of responsible scriptural reading for subsequent generations; and third, from this, by offering some tentative conclusions about the significance of relationally responsible readings of Scripture for a contemporary doctrine of *sola scriptura*, identifying the necessity of reading Scripture through the creeds and symbols in order that Scripture can form the community of the church as a community under the authority of Jesus Christ.

THE IMPORTANCE OF THE HIERARCHICAL PRIORITY OF SCRIPTURE OVER TRADITION

Over and against progressive, developmental understandings of church dogma, which exist under the authority of the church that also defines the canon and offers its (singular and sometimes new) true interpretation,[5] the magisterial Protestant tradition advocates the principle of *sola scriptura*. John Calvin, following Augustine,[6] rightly points out that it is more appropriate to render the A.D. 381 creed's clause on the church "I believe the church" than it is to render it "I believe in the church," in order to differentiate between the object of faith and the means of knowing faith—that is, between God in whom Christians place their faith, and the church that makes this God known.[7] The church is not the locus of faith for the individual,

---

[5]Cf. John Henry Newman, *An Essay on the Development of Christian Doctrine* (London: Penguin, 1974).

[6]Augustine, *On Faith and the Creed*, 10.21, Nicene and Post-Nicene Fathers series 3, 331. This recognizes the difference between the use of *eis* in Eusebius's *Ecclesiatical History* and in *The Acts of the Council of Chalcedon*.

[7]John Calvin, *Institutes of the Christian Religion*, trans. Ford Lewis Battles (Louisville: Westminster John Knox, 1960), II.1013.

but the temporal and spatial body that directs the believer in her faith in God.

Crucially, one implication of this seems to be, however, that it is also inappropriate to state that we believe *in* Scripture: it is appropriate for the believer to believe Scripture that makes the God of salvation known, but not *in* Scripture as itself the saving object. It is because faith is appropriately located in Christ alone (*solus Christus*) that the Reformers advocate that Scripture governs and rules the church, since Christ is to be *discovered* in the testimony of the witnesses to the encounter with him. There is an important hierarchy to be noted here. As Karl Barth puts it:

> In the 16th century . . . the Evangelical [*Evangelisch*] decision was taken that the Church has not to seek and find the Word and authority of Jesus Christ except where He Himself has established it, that it and its word and authority can derive only from the word and authority of the biblical witnesses, that its word and authority are always confronted by those of the biblical witnesses, and are measured and must be judged by them. This is what the Reformation was trying to say and did say in its affirmation that Holy Scripture alone has divine authority in the Church. It was not ascribing a godlike value to the book as a book and the letter as a letter—in some sinister antithesis to spirit, and power and life. But it wanted Jesus Christ to be known and acknowledged as the Lord of the Church, whose revelation would not have been revelation if it had not created apostles and prophets, and even in the present-day Church can only be revelation in this its primary sign.[8]

The hierarchy we see is this: Christ as sovereign over Scripture, and Scripture as sovereign over the church. But this hierarchy does not exist in such a way that the revelation of the Word of God does not confront the believer in the church. Instead, it points to the mediated revelation of

---

[8]Karl Barth, *Church Dogmatics* (Edinburgh: T & T Clark, 1936–1977), I.2, p. 581.

God in the church through Scripture:[9] Scripture is, according to Barth, "the sign of a sign," and only in reading this "sign of a sign" can the church hear the apostles and prophets, in order to hear and meet Jesus Christ.[10] Since Jesus Christ is the sovereign Lord of the church, it is only under Scripture (which testifies to Christ), and by being obedient to Scripture, that the church has authority; and this authority is a humble and mediated authority through Scripture, rather than an authority that might appeal to Christ and the Holy Spirit directly in support of its beliefs and actions without recourse to the Bible.[11] Thus, both because the authority of Scripture derives from its testimony to Jesus Christ, and because the believer truly confronts Jesus Christ in the church and only in Scripture do we learn about Jesus Christ, Scripture rules over the church.

When we come, therefore, to creeds and symbols, we must note that their authority is an authority that exists *under* Scripture rather than over Scripture. This is an issue that the Reformers are at pains to emphasize. Calvin advocates that the very right of councils to gather and claim any authority rests in the promise of Scripture that where two or three are gathered, Christ will be present.[12] Furthermore, the judgments of councils are authoritative only because they are based solely on Scripture,[13] and these judgments are therefore meaningful, by virtue of this, not only in the contexts in which they take place, but also now and in the future, since the church still stands under the authority of Scripture.[14] Councils, symbols and creeds are, therefore, exercises in biblical interpretation, in hermeneutics.[15] Furthermore, from a Prot-

---

[9]On ecclesial mediation in Barth, see John Yocum, *Ecclesial Mediation in Karl Barth* (Aldershot, UK: Ashgate, 2004).

[10]Barth, *Church Dogmatics*, I.2, p. 583.

[11]Ibid., p. 586.

[12]Calvin, *Institutes*, II.1166-67.

[13]Ibid., II.1178.

[14]Ibid., II.1173.

[15]In this way, I wish to draw a stronger demarcation than Pannenberg does between Scripture and tradition; see Pannenberg, *Basic Questions in Theology, Volume 1*, p. 186. However, I agree with his argument later in the same piece that "later tradition is viewed not as completing the content of Scripture, but as having a purely hermeneutical function" (p. 188).

estant perspective, they are relationally responsible exercises in hermeneutics, in which the church universally (catholically) engages, and
whether councils are correct in their decisions rests on the appropri-
ateness of their biblical interpretation.[16] It is to this that we now turn.

COUNCILS ARE EXERCISES IN RELATIONALLY RESPONSIBLE HERMENEUTICS

Much recent patristic scholarship has pointed to the priority of scriptural
interpretation for the theology of the fathers and in conciliar debates and
statements. As Lewis Ayres makes clear in his work, the fourth century
saw debates about the explication of the (so-called) plain sense of
Scripture, with theological argument about the best way to explicate
Scripture and the best philosophical and terminological resources to do
so.[17] For the fathers, there were not differing disciplines with differing data
on which to reflect (be that systematic theology, history, philosophy or
the Bible); there was only the task of reflecting on the narrative of Scripture
and the best way in which to express from that the grammar of the divine.[18]
In this, to borrow terminology from George Lindbeck, the governing vo-
cabulary lexical core was Scripture as the locus in which the narrative of
salvation was to be found and the God of that salvation was to be known.[19]

The centrality of biblical interpretation to the decisions, creeds and
symbols of the first four councils determines in the first instance that
Scripture is the yardstick (*kanon*) by which all decisions of councils are
measured, and the basis on which they are made. Thus, even when
councils seem to make statements that are not contained in Scripture,
they do so arising out of the activity of offering a condensed interpre-

---

[16]Cf. Calvin, *Institutes*, II.1176-79. For the Reformers, it is key that the councils can be wrong.

[17]Lewis Ayres, *Nicea and Its Legacy: An Approach to Fourth-Century Trinitarian Theology* (Oxford: Oxford University Press, 2004), esp. pp. 38-40; cf. David Yeago, "The New Testament and Nicene Dogma," *Pro Ecclesia* 3 (1994): 152-64.

[18]See here, Ayres, *Nicea and Its Legacy*, pp. 14-15; cf. George A. Lindbeck, *The Nature of Doctrine: Religion and Theology in a Postliberal Age* (London: SPCK, 1982), esp. pp. 79-84.

[19]Lindbeck, *Nature of Doctrine*, p. 81.

tation of or coda on Scripture. For example, Calvin asks those who argue that the term *consubstantial* is not found in Scripture: "What else are the Nicene fathers doing when they declare them [the Father and the Son] of one essence but simply expounding the real meaning of Scripture?"[20] For both Calvin and Luther, the role of councils is not to *create* doctrine, but to *preserve* the teachings of Scripture as understood by the church and to refute heresy:[21] councils, for them, simply state what the Scriptures say. Again, to quote Calvin:

> We willingly embrace and reverence as holy the early councils . . . which were concerned with refuting errors—in so far as they relate to the teachings of faith. For they [the councils] contain nothing but the pure and genuine exposition of Scripture, which the holy fathers applied with spiritual prudence to crush the enemies of religion who had arisen.[22]

This is a point that is also made repeatedly by Luther in his treatise *On the Councils and the Church*. In this, Luther argues that councils do not do anything new, but only confirm inherited truth from Scripture against heresies and innovations. His argument thereby reduces the authority of councils, since they do not innovate in terms of doctrine but only confirm what is already in Scripture. Since the four principal councils did not innovate, according to Luther's interpretation, in terms of church teaching, the church presently cannot do so.[23]

Even if contemporary historiography determines that we can no longer take such a view of the history of orthodoxy and heresy,[24] two

---

[20]Calvin, *Institutes*, II.1165.

[21]This is, indeed, how the fathers understood themselves. See, for example, Athanasius, *Contra Arianos*.

[22]Calvin, *Institutes*, II.1171-72. Luther makes a parallel argument about the condensing of the biblical narrative into the term *homoousios*; see Martin Luther, *On the Councils and the Church*, in Eric W. Gitsch, ed., *Church and Ministry III*, Luther's Works vol. 41 (Philadelphia: Fortress, 1966), p. 83.

[23]See Luther, *On the Councils and the Church*, pp. 9-178.

[24]See on this, for example, Walter Bauer, *Orthodoxy and Heresy in Earliest Christianity* (Philadelphia: Fortress, 1971).

important points should be made here. First, the Reformers correctly identify the centrality of biblical interpretation performed relationally to the decisions of councils, and—in this—the Reformers recognize the authority of Scripture over councils. Second, the Reformers identify a key relational aspect to this means of interpretation: the way in which one reads the biblical narrative becomes the determining feature of the identity of the church. Despite historiographical issues, the theological, ecclesial and hermeneutical points still stand: to be a part of the one, holy, catholic and apostolic church means reading Scripture with that church in a particular way, and in a way that will determine the minimal parameters in which subsequent readings will take place within that community. Indeed, modern critical historiography may in fact add support to the case being made here (and there are many of them): out of various interpretative options, the holy, catholic and apostolic church identifies itself in relation to the particular interpretative framework it finds most compelling and scriptural; the issues at stake between what we might refer to anachronistically as orthodox and heterodox communities are hermeneutical in the formation of their identities.

Let us consider these two points in a little more detail. First, in understanding the councils as relational exercises in biblical hermeneutics, we see the fathers as engaging in negotiated, ecclesial and catholic interpretations of Scripture for the church. That these interpretations are enacted relationally is of central concern to the Protestant tradition. Calvin points to the fact that councils and synods arise out of a crisis or in order to solve a major issue through *common* deliberation. It is the very collectivity of the decisions of the pastors about the interpretation of Scripture that gives the decision weight, in comparison to the decisions and findings of a few individuals with regard to scriptural interpretation.[25] For Luther, we know the truth of these conciliar decisions because the sheep (i.e., the whole body of the church) recognize the voice of Christ. Thus, the whole church engages together in judgment

---

[25]Calvin, *Institutes*, II.1176-77.

on the appropriate interpretation of texts by virtue of the church's affirmation of what is true in their acceptance of creeds and symbols: it is not that bishops and councils judge the church, but that all Christians judge the truthfulness of the claims of councils. Symbols and creeds are supreme exercises, therefore, in relational responsibility in hermeneutics since they involve the *whole* church's (in the broadest and plainest sense) reading of Scripture, taking the power of interpretation away from bishops and scholars, and placing the responsibility in the hands of the entire church. Thus, writes Luther: "Bishops, popes, scholars, and everyone else have the power to teach, but it is the sheep who are to judge whether they teach the voice [i.e., the words] of Christ or the voice of strangers."[26] In this sense, *sola scriptura* is a fundamentally relational-hermeneutical account both of the authority of councils under Scripture (through the church's common interpretation of Scripture), and of the authority of creedal statements in relation to the church. There is a cycle here: Scripture is the authority on which the symbol and creed rest as it is negotiated by those at the councils; this authority is recognized by the broader body of the church, whose collective assent is the true catholicity of the creedal or symbolic formula.

This relates to the second issue—that the way in which one reads the biblical narrative becomes the determining feature of the identity of the church. Here, the issue is not primarily that creeds offer dense narratives of the *sensus plenior* of Scripture in relation to the central character of God, Father, Son and Holy Spirit, though this is certainly part of the story. The issue is more that creeds offer means to help to prevent getting the references of Scripture wrong, or more appropriately offer minimal frameworks in which the references of Scripture might be understood and interpreted. Councils were—in one sense—about com-

---

[26]Martin Luther, *That a Christian Assembly or Congregation Has the Right and Power to Judge All Teaching and to Call, Appoint, and Dismiss Teachers, Established and Proven by Scripture*, in Eric W. Gritsch, ed., *Church and Ministry I*, Luther's Works vol. 93 (Philadelphia: Fortress, 1970), p. 307 (cf. pp. 305-14); cf. Luther, *On the Councils and the Church*, p. 61, where Luther argues that we can identify past heresy because it died away, and the church universal did not recognize it.

munity formation and identity in relation to the parameters of the interpretation of Scriptural texts.[27] In terms of their contemporary use in relation to biblical interpretation, creeds and symbols continue to set the relationally responsible means of interpreting Scripture for the community that identifies itself as part of the one, holy, catholic and apostolic church. Thus, creeds and symbols are not only formed relationally, but they continue to form the relationality that exists within the church in terms of the minimal parameters they set for biblical interpretation. To quote Thiselton on tradition: "It yields, in Wittgenstein's language, sufficient regularities of beliefs and practices to offer an identifiable continuity within the public world, but sufficient development, change, and particularity to allow for the growth of new sociolinguistic horizons as new socio-historical contexts emerge."[28] Thus, the relational effect of creedal and symbolic interpretation of biblical texts is the formation of a community identity shaped around a shared set of minimal parameters for the reading of Scripture: hermeneutics shapes the relational identity of the church, and the relational identity of the church shapes the way the church continues to read the Holy Bible. Crucially, however, this second point cannot be held without the first point: the authority of symbols and creeds rests on their interpretation of Scripture that is affirmed by the universal catholicity of the entire church (i.e., all of its members; we note well here the baptismal use of the Niceno-Constantinopolitan creed). With Barth, we must say first about any church confession that "its authority is simply its content as scriptural exposition, which is necessarily confirmed or judged by Scripture itself."[29] But we need to say in the same breath the following: "To make a confession, *confiteri*, is to proclaim its content, to publish it, to make it known, to make it known as widely and universally as possible. A confession demands publicity. This derives from its nature as

---

[27]See Frances Young, *The Making of the Creeds* (London: SCM, 2002), pp. xiv, 14.

[28]Anthony C. Thiselton, *New Horizons in Hermeneutics: The Theory and Practice of Transforming Biblical Reading* (Grand Rapids: Zondervan, 1992), p. 9.

[29]Barth, *Church Dogmatics*, I.2, p. 638.

the word of the whole Church to the whole Church."[30] A relational interpretation of Scripture is affirmed by the full relationality of the church, and forms the minimal parameters of the church in relation to its interpretation of biblical texts.[31]

PROVISIONAL CONCLUSIONS: SOME IMPLICATIONS FOR A CONTEMPORARY DOCTRINE OF *SOLA SCRIPTURA*

Put in the starkest terms, what I am trying to argue is that within the community that identifies itself in relation to this particular relational hermeneutic of creedal and symbolic statements, a true doctrine of *sola scriptura* demands that Scripture is read through creedal and symbolic statements in the way outlined thus far within this chapter. This is because *sola scriptura* is a doctrine concerning the *church's* relationship to the sovereignty of Scripture over it *before* it is a doctrine of the *individual's* relationship to Scripture: the latter only arises out of the former, as the former concerns the "public" reading of Scripture.[32] Luther famously puts the matter thus:

> Whenever you hear or see this word preached, believed, professed, and lived, do not doubt that the true *ecclesia sancta catholica*, "a Christian holy people" must be there ... for God's word cannot be without God's people, and conversely, God's people cannot be without God's word. Otherwise, who would preach or hear it preached, if there were no people of God?[33]

The Word of God stands in a hierarchical relationship to the church, which is formed by it and derives its authority from Scripture. But this Word is known only with a terminus of encounter—only within the re-

---

[30]Ibid., p. 639.

[31]The issue of *church* interpretation is obviously important here. I am deliberately focusing this on the community of interpretation of the church. Outside of this community, these parameters hold no sway, and a much broader range of interpretations are possible. But *within the community that interprets Scripture this way*, creeds and symbols set this parameter.

[32]Calvin points to the dangers of private reading of Scripture without the church; see, for example, *Institutes*, II.1018.

[33]Luther, *On the Councils and the Church*, p. 150.

lationality of God's people, the church. Paul Tillich is quite wrong, therefore, when he states: "It is a demonic and therefore destructive act for the community of faith to be interpreted as unconditional subjection to the doctrinal statements of faith as they have developed in the rather ambiguous history of the churches."[34] It is the very identity of the church in relation to the interpretation of Scripture that concerns the statements of creeds and symbols; it is out of the authority of Scripture that these statements arise; and it is because of the relationality of the church that such statements are made catholically. In one sense, ambiguity is the very point: creedal and symbolic statements arise to give identity to the community of the church in relation to its reading of Scripture *within* the ambiguity of history, and they continue to provide a relational hermeneutic in changing contexts of interpretation. These statements connect the church's interpretation of Scripture not only to the geographical breadth of the catholic church, but to the historical communion of saints of all ages—past, present and future.[35] Barth puts this matter well:

> Just because the Evangelical [*Evangelisch*] confession is a confession of the vitality and the presence of God's Word actualised again and again, it is also a confession of the communion of saints and therefore of what is, in a sense, an authoritative tradition of the Word of God, that is, of a human form in which that Word comes to all those who are summoned by it to faith and witness in the sphere of the Church and by its mouth.[36]

This is not an independent authority of a tradition over Scripture, but a subordination of the *entire* church in its relationality to Scripture. Barth also states:

> Ecclesiastical history can be heard and respected as ecclesiastical authority only when there is discussion on the basis of a common

---

[34]Paul Tillich, *Systematic Theology* (Digswell Place, UK: James Nisbet, 1968), 3:186.
[35]Pannenberg explores this in relation to continuity into the future; see *Basic Questions in Theology, Volume 1*, pp. 205-9.
[36]Barth, *Church Dogmatics*, I.2, p. 573.

hearing and receiving of the Word of God, and in that discussion one of those agreements, and in the documenting of that agreement a common confession, in matters of faith—hence, only when answers are given to the question of a true faith by way of speech and counter-speech, agreement and a common declaration in the face of Holy Scripture.[37]

In recognizing that the church confronts Jesus Christ in Scripture in every age, the believer must seek to orientate her reading of Scripture relationally onto the relational readings of Scripture that have taken place throughout the history of the church in the statements of the first four councils.

Sola scriptura is ultimately, therefore, a relational account of the way in which Scripture is read. If the believer wishes to recognize the authority of Scripture over the church, it is meaningless for her to read Scripture to this end *extra muros ecclesiae*. For that reason, her reading must be relationally responsible to the catholicity of the communion of saints if it is to be orientated toward understanding Scripture as authoritative over the life of the church. In the continuation of history, in all its contingency, to proclaim a belief in *sola scriptura* is not to proclaim a belief in individual autonomy in relation to the biblical text, but to proclaim a belief in the sovereignty of Christ, who is known only through Scripture, over *the body of the church*. This is what the true humility of the present Protestant churches must be, as the church seeks to stand under Scripture alone, a present-day catholic church made up of individuals related to one another in Christ, and seeking to hear in Scripture the proclamation of Christ to the church of which he is the head in all places and times.[38]

In seeking to read Scripture relationally within the communion of saints of all places and times through sharing in the interpretation of the first four councils, the church will begin to discover the true hier-

---

[37]Ibid., p. 594.
[38]Cf. ibid., p. 693.

archy of relations of authority. This is ultimately in terms of the sovereignty of the true God. While symbolic and creedal statements may seem to offer ever more technical, precise and fine-grained accounts of the nature of the trinitarian God, their purpose is to provide this definition for the communion of believers in order to prevent idolatry,[39] or as Nicholas Lash puts it, "of getting the reference wrong: of taking that to be God which is not God, of making some fact or thing or nation or person or dream or possession or ideal for our heart's desire and the mystery 'that moves the sun and other stars.'"[40] The process of symbolic and creedal formulation is one of seeking from Scripture the proper reference for "God" in the narrative of God's encounter with creation, and in this, that reference is made more (and not less) mysterious.[41] The relational responsibility of individual believers in connection to Scriptural hermeneutics is not about the aggregation of power to the church; it is rather—even in its most detailed and confident claims—about the humility of the church ultimately before the God of our salvation; before Jesus Christ; before the testimony of prophets and apostles who bear witness to him; and before the body of Christ of which each individual is only ever one part. *Sola scriptura* as a doctrine seeks that proper ordering, and for that reason is meaningful in the church, and to individuals within the church only in their relation to one another and ultimately to God: in *sola scriptura*, therefore, one might hope to find a truly relationally responsible mode of biblical hermeneutics.

---

[39]Cf. Frances Young, *The Making of the Creeds*, p. 103.
[40]Nicholas Lash, *The Beginning and End of "Religion"* (Cambridge: Cambridge University Press, 1996), p. 134.
[41]Cf. Williams, *Arius*, p. 236.

8

Biblical Hermeneutics
and *Ecclesial* Responsibility

R. Walter L. Moberly

INTRODUCTION

One of the abiding memories of my reading theology in Cambridge in the mid-seventies, as part of my training for ordination, is the regularity with which I, and at least some others, moaned to the then-principal of our college that we could not see how the biblical work that we did in our lectures and essays related to what we would need to do with the Bible in our preaching and pastoral ministry. It was all very well to write an essay on, say, the authorship of the Pastoral Epistles; but if one decided that the balance of evidence pointed against Pauline authorship, and that evidence for the acceptability of pseudonymity in early Christianity was inconclusive, what was one to do? Should one preface one's sermon with "Although the text claims to have been written by Paul, it probably wasn't, and so it probably isn't trustworthy"? And what about the numerous first-person passages, especially in 2 Timothy ("I am reminded of your sincere faith"; "I know the one in whom I have put my trust"; "what persecutions I endured"; "Alexander the coppersmith did me great harm"; 2 Tim. 1:5, 12; 3:11; 4:14)? Should one explain that this is apparently the voice of an imposter, and so not to be believed? To the best of my memory, lectures in the divinity faculty gave little or no help with the question of what one should *do* with the fruits of one's biblical scholarship in the context of contemporary Christian faith.

Within the theological college there was a one-term course in the final year, "Use of the Bible," which was somehow meant to address (and resolve?) the issues. In the event, the course simply involved reading and discussing some essays about the authority of Scripture from a variety of viewpoints, with no help at all on practical questions (such as: How should I preach the Pastorals?). So the simplest thing to do (I speak for myself at that time) was to play safe and argue that the Pastorals must really have been written by Paul, as otherwise their integrity was impugned. To be sure, I was uneasy with this approach: how could I genuinely evaluate issues of language and thought in the Pastorals in relation to undoubted Pauline letters, if I knew in advance what the answer had to be? But I could see no clear alternative, and I felt committed to such a stance as a matter of ecclesial faithfulness, indeed responsibility (though I probably wouldn't have called it that at the time).

Thankfully, things have changed since then. Now any student has ready access to a wide range of conceptual tools drawn from work in hermeneutics, tools that enable constructive rethinking and reframing of the puzzles of biblical criticism; and this is substantially due, at least within the UK, to the work of Anthony Thiselton, in whose honor this volume was first initiated. However, there is no room for complacency. Dale Martin, in his recent book *Pedagogy of the Bible*,[1] finds the way the Bible is taught in divinity schools and seminaries in the US to be not fit for purpose—future leaders of churches, who will spend much time reading and interpreting biblical texts, can finish their studies and still be relatively clueless about how to handle these texts well in the situations in which they will find themselves (as I too was). So there is still work to be done!

---

[1]Dale B. Martin, *Pedagogy of the Bible: An Analysis and Proposal* (Louisville and London: Westminster John Knox, 2008).

ECCLESIAL RESPONSIBILITY: A THIN ACCOUNT

The notion of ecclesial responsibility was not alien to my Cambridge teachers. To the best of my knowledge, all were Christian believers, and most of them were ordained ministers in their respective denominations. Nonetheless, within an academic context their account of ecclesial responsibility in relationship to biblical study would, I think, have been distinctly limited. I suspect that they would have been in substantial agreement with John Barton in his 1992 inaugural lecture as Oriel and Laing Professor at Oxford, where he with characteristic elegance expounds what is arguably *the* paradigm of modern academic biblical study.[2]

Barton recognizes the appeal of contemporary proposals that "the interpreter of Scripture should operate with a set of hermeneutical principles which will make the reading of the text *fruitful* for theology and religious faith"[3]; but he regards these as siren voices that will lure the enterprise of biblical scholarship onto the rocks. The reason for this is simple. It threatens to undermine the principle of *criticism*, and thereby undermine scholarly *freedom*. "To put it simply, the Bible is read critically where it is believed that its meaning can be determined only by unprejudiced investigation, and is not known from tradition, through ecclesiastical authority, or by applying certain hermeneutical rules."[4] Barton acknowledges that a "determination to understand [the biblical text] for oneself, independently of the Church's traditional exegesis"[5] is a child of the Enlightenment (one without difficulty hears the tones of Immanuel Kant's *aude sapere*, "dare to think for yourself"). But he sees it as no less a child of the deepest instincts of Protestantism. The

---

[2]John Barton, *The Future of Old Testament Study* (Oxford: Oxford University Press, 1993). In his subsequent *The Nature of Biblical Criticism* (Louisville and London: Westminster John Knox, 2007), Barton develops the thesis more fully without changing its substance. I have offered a fuller critique in my "Biblical Criticism and Religious Belief," *Journal of Theological Interpretation* 2, no. 1 (2008): 71-100.

[3]Barton, *Future of Old Testament Study*, p. 7.

[4]Ibid., p. 9.

[5]Ibid., p. 11.

point is that biblical criticism "is part of a quest for truth,"[6] and so its practitioners ought to keep their eyes on that goal, rather than on traditional ecclesial authority or understandings—otherwise how far would Martin Luther have got? "If biblical scholars who are Christians do have special obligations to their fellow believers, then these (it seems to me) are not discharged by feeding the churches with 'edifying' or 'reverent' scholarship, but by freeing people from authorities and traditions that usurp their own right to ask for themselves what the Bible means."[7] In short, the task of Christian biblical scholars is to keep the churches honest, by refusing to let them hear from the Bible only what they want to hear. Let others do what they will with the findings of biblical scholarship—freedom is a gift always liable to abuse. But possible anxieties about uses of scholarly findings of which one might disapprove should not deter biblical scholars from their quest for truth.

That one should be patiently, scrupulously and (as far as is possible) dispassionately attentive to the meaning of the biblical text is, as far as it goes, unarguable. Also, the need to be honest, and to have a healthy recognition of how easily preferences and prejudices can cloud vision, is likewise unarguable. Yet I want to call this a *thin* account of the ecclesial responsibility of the biblical scholar, because of the number of concerns it does not address, that it potentially skews, or that it prematurely takes for granted. For example, although the scholarly practice of my student self clearly falls foul of Barton's critique, precisely because it was (on a charitable reading!) showing undue concern for "traditional ecclesial authority or understandings," I think that nonetheless there is a certain mismatch between my practice and his critique.

On the one hand, the rhetoric of establishing for oneself what the Bible means surely bears little relation to the realities of student learning. What is usually at stake, at least in discussion of authorship of biblical books, is that one should come to accept an antecedent scholarly consensus, which often differs from a traditional ecclesial understanding.

---

[6]Ibid.
[7]Ibid., p. 12.

Of course, reasons are given why one should accept that consensus, and one is free to make counterarguments. But how many beginning students have sufficient facility in ancient history and philological analysis to genuinely work out difficult issues for themselves? The challenge for the student can feel less like pioneering philological honesty than like a question of willingness to give allegiance to a scholarly community, whose self-identity tends to be cast in terms of its arguments being empirical, nondogmatic and open to revision, and so apparently different from the ecclesial.[8]

On the other hand, my reservations about non-Pauline authorship were, I think, less philological than existential. Encountering the scholarly consensus felt like being told that an old and trusted friend was not really trustworthy. My imagination related less to trajectories of ecclesial development in early Christianity (now apparently clarified) than to the world of the "Pauline" text (now apparently spurious). My reservations about non-Pauline authorship expressed in philological terms were really rationalizations of other concerns. To be sure, this can simply be taken as a good example of the problem that worries Barton— that is, it simply exemplifies the way in which "presuppositions of faith stifle honest communication,"[9] and so need to be bracketed if scholarly work is to be truly scholarly. Moreover, I have no great desire to uphold the thought-world of my student self. Nonetheless, it may be that a scholarly paradigm of biblical study that has nothing (apparently) to say about questions of identity, allegiance, life practices or trust, other than that they are in principle irrelevant, is itself open to question. In other words, it is surely a paradigm rooted in a certain kind of classic liberal

---

[8]For a telling account of scholarly induction as often entailing a kind of "conversion narrative," see Jon Levenson, "Historical Criticism and the Fate of the Enlightenment Project," in his *The Hebrew Bible, the Old Testament, and Historical Criticism* (Louisville: Westminster John Knox, 1993), pp. 106-26, esp. pp. 106-10.

[9]This wording is from Michael Fox's recent statement of an approach similar to that of John Barton: "Scholarship and Faith in Bible Study," in Roland Boer, ed., *Secularism and Biblical Studies* (London and Oakville, CT: Equinox, 2010), p. 17. This is a revision of an earlier 2006 online essay in the Society of Biblical Literature forum, which received considerable publicity (www.sbl-site.org/Article.aspx?ArticleId=490).

individualism, which considers faith as essentially an optional cognitive attribute of an individual, and which presupposes but does not usually scrutinize certain sociopolitical and institutional arrangements. By contrast, recent hermeneutics has, among other things, probed the social nature of knowledge, where faith can be considered in terms of institutional arrangements, tacit assumptions, linguistic conventions and corporate practices (not instead of, but as well as, individual appropriations and expressions of faith).

More generally, it is important to take seriously the changing cultural context within which Christian biblical scholars, even in secular universities, are located. As Nicholas Lash has put it (in expounding Karl Rahner):

> In a Christian culture, a culture in which scholarly attentiveness goes hand in hand with contemplation, a culture quite at ease with prayer, it is society as a whole that sings the song, that makes the music. In such a society, it is quite in order for the academic theologian simply to function as *technician*—as music critic, we might say, or as historian of musicology. However, in a culture such as ours (and, for this purpose, it matters not whether we call it "secular" or "pagan")—a culture lacking in contemplativity, finding prayerfulness a *problem*—in such a culture, *no* Christian can afford the luxury of sitting in the audience, but *all* are called to sing the song, to make the music of the Gospel.[10]

A certain time-honored bracketing of ecclesial identity for the Christian biblical scholar qua biblical scholar may have become a luxury that can no longer be afforded.

ECCLESIAL RESPONSIBILITY:
THE IMPLICATIONS OF THE CANON

Setting the scene. By way of trying to articulate a thicker account of ec-

---

[10]"Creation, Courtesy and Contemplation," in Nicholas Lash, *The Beginning and the End of "Religion"* (Cambridge: Cambridge University Press, 1996), pp. 175-76.

clesial responsibility, I want to focus on renewed scholarly interest in the biblical canon. Although this interest has often taken the form of various kinds of *historical* enquiry (both as to the development of the biblical canon in itself, and as to the ways in which the developments of religious thought and practice in Israel and the early church most likely differed from the way they are presented in the canon), my concern here is with the potential *hermeneutical* significance of the canon. I will use *canon* as a convenient shorthand for a range of interrelated concerns[11] to do with the nature of religiously authoritative texts—i.e., the phenomenon of Scripture[12]—in the context of biblical study.

A preliminary clarification. I am not unaware of the contemporary suspicions directed by some scholars to the phenomenon of canon as primarily a sophisticated code for power games (the control of some and the exclusion of others), nor would I deny that there has indeed been practical warrant for such suspicions. Interestingly, such ideological suspicion can have significant common ground with John Barton's concerns. As George Aichele puts it: "The canon of the Bible is, among other things, an oppressive ideological institution, one that *prevents* people from reading these diverse and ambiguous books or that so controls the reading of these texts that people are in effect blinded and crippled by the canonical constraints."[13] This, however, makes it the more important to try to clarify what kind of epistemology and practices the phenomenon of the biblical canon does, and does not, entail.[14]

---

[11]There are numerous debates attached to the different ways in which *canon* can be used, a valuable guide to which is Stephen B. Chapman, "The Canon Debate: What It Is and Why It Matters," *Journal of Theological Interpretation* 4, no. 2 (2010): pp. 273-94.

[12]A helpful guide to the issues posed by the phenomenon of Scripture is Wilfred Cantwell Smith, *What Is Scripture? A Comparative Approach* (London: SCM, 1993).

[13]George Aichele, *The Control of Biblical Meaning: Canon as Semiotic Mechanism* (Harrisburg, PA: TPI, 2001), p. 226. David Clines comparably questions the continuing value of the category of a "classic," because "classics" are "chosen in the interests of a hegemonic class, who have had the authority to declare certain works classics and others not" ("Reading the Song of Songs as a Classic," in David J. A. Clines and Ellen van Wolde, eds., *A Critical Engagement: Essays on the Hebrew Bible in Honour of J. Cheryl Exum*, Hebrew Bible Monographs 38 [Sheffield, UK: Sheffield Phoenix, 2011], p. 130.)

[14]Throughout this discussion I am using *biblical canon* and *Bible* for the Christian Bible of

It is well known that the Christian canon of Scripture was formed in the early centuries of the church at the same time as the church was developing its creeds, its liturgies, its leadership and its rule of faith. Moreover Christian scholars, whose sermons and commentaries gave guidance for the general ecclesial construal of Scripture, were also beginning to emerge. All these processes were contested, as the identity of the catholic church was steadily articulated through constant engagement with numerous other options within the life and thought of late antiquity. My approach here is not to reconsider that history, but rather to ask, in a preliminary way, what form such issues might take in a contemporary context.

One presupposition of the discussion that follows from the analogy with the early centuries is that Bible and church are correlative notions—the one needs and depends on the other. It is still difficult to escape the legacy of the sixteenth century's polarizing of these over against each other ("Which is more authoritative?" "Which comes first?") and to find fresh ways of expressing their interrelatedness; but that is the task. The other presupposition is that Bible and theology are also correlative notions—the one needs and depends on the other. It is likewise still difficult to escape the legacy of eighteenth- and nineteenth-century polarization of biblical study over against dogmatic theology,[15] and to find fresh ways to express their interrelatedness; but that too is the task. The points that follow are a preliminary outline of what that complex task entails, in a way that seeks, downwind of modernity, to articulate how we might do now what the fathers of the church did then.

Canon and the keeping together of discrete documents. First, canon represents the decision to *collate and preserve certain documents in a par-*

---

both Old and New Testaments, without prejudice to the issues posed by the biblical canon in a Jewish frame of reference.

[15]The landmark account, to which appeal is routinely made, is J. P. Gabler, "On the Proper Distinction Between Biblical and Dogmatic Theology and the Specific Objectives of Each" (1787), which is conveniently available in J. Sandys-Wunsch and L. Eldredge, "J. P. Gabler and the Distinction Between Biblical and Systematic Theology: Translation, Commentary, and Discussion of His Originality," *Scottish Journal of Theology* 33 (1980): 133-58.

ticular unitary collection, which Christians have historically put within a single codex, or book. We are perhaps so accustomed to publishers being happy to publish the canonical collection that we can easily take it for granted. But why should Israel's Scriptures be a bounded collection, in which Deuteronomy and Ecclesiastes belong together, Ben Sira may or may not belong, and *Jubilees* does not belong? Why should the Scriptures of the early church be a bounded collection, in which John's Gospel, 2 Peter and Revelation belong, but the *Gospel of Thomas,* the *Didache* and the apostolic fathers do not? And why should Israel's Scriptures become the first part of a book that culminates with early Christian Scriptures, such that together these collections become Old and New Testaments, the Christian Bible? As Robert Jenson puts it:

> Apart from the canon's role as a collection of texts the church assembled to serve its specific needs, the volume comprising the canon is not a plausible literary or historical unit. . . . Apart from the fact that Israel's Scripture funded the initial church, and apart from the fact that the church collected writings of its own in one book with this Scripture, there would have been no "Holy Bible," and there would be no reason to treat the documents now bound together under that title as anything but sundry relics of two or more ancient Mideastern religions. It is only because the church maintains the collection of these documents, with the texts they presented, as the book she needs, that we are concerned for their interpretation.[16]

Or, as he puts it in an earlier account of the same point:

> Protestantism emphasizes that these precise documents *impose* themselves on the church; Catholicism East and West emphasizes that it is the *church* that recognizes the exigency. I mean only to make the simple point presupposed by and included in both emphases: the collection comes together in and for the church.

Where the church's calling to speak the gospel is not shared,

---

[16]Robert W. Jenson, *Canon and Creed* (Louisville: Westminster John Knox, 2010), p. 55.

the binding of these particular documents between one cover becomes a historical accident of no hermeneutical significance.[17]

In short, *canon* signifies that a particular and contestable collection
of documents belong together, and so should be interpreted together, in
a way that contributes to forming the frame of reference and hermeneutical priorities of the Christian biblical scholar.

Canon and the privileging of biblical documents. Secondly, to canonize documents means *to privilege* them. It is a way of saying that the
texts that constitute the Bible have a significance that other texts do not
have. Canon is a shorthand for the *value,* and also the *authority,* of the
documents that constitute the Bible. It is a way of saying that in this
literary deposit of the religion of Israel and the early church there is an
enduring value that is not to be found in other religions of the ancient
Mediterranean world and their remains.[18] This is not a necessary
judgment, to be justified by abstract rational criteria (e.g., the once-
common Enlightenment appeal to the intrinsic philosophical superiority of monotheistic belief), but is a particular judgment, dependent
on past decisions by Jews and Christians and their continuing recognition today. Absent that continuing acknowledgement of Jewish and
Christian judgments, it is difficult to justify giving more attention to the
biblical documents (other than in terms of Western cultural studies)
than to any other religious or philosophical texts from antiquity. The
issues here are analogous to those to do with classics, where widespread
and sustained recognition is necessary for a work to be considered a
classic, and where the increasingly disparate nature of contemporary
culture makes increasingly contested the issue of which works qualify
as classics, and why.

---

[17]Robert W. Jenson, "Hermeneutics and the Life of the Church," in Carl E. Braaten and
Robert W. Jenson, eds., *Reclaiming the Bible for the Church* (Edinburgh: T & T Clark,
1995), p. 89.
[18]This is not, or at least need not be, a dismissive judgment about that which is not privileged
("light here, darkness there"), even though it is a strong judgment about relative and enduring value.

It has, of course, been regularly pointed out that for the task of understanding the religious thought of the ancient Near East or the Hellenistic world, such canonical compilation, privileging and demarcating represents subsequent value judgments that should form no part of the frame of reference of the historian of the period in which the documents were originally written.[19] More recently it has become common to argue that the biblical voices may have been unrepresentative of their time and place and so any privileging of them should be set aside also in the name of justice and scholarly integrity so as to enable voices marginalized by the biblical voices to be heard on their own terms.[20] Such critiques make it imperative to clarify afresh what the privileging of the canonical documents does, and does not, entail. A strong account of what is potentially at stake for Christians is offered by Andrew Louth:

> We become Christians by becoming members of the Church, by *trusting* our forefathers in the faith. If we cannot trust the Church to have understood Jesus, then we have lost Jesus: and the resources of modern scholarship will not help us to find him.[21]

Unsurprisingly, for a variety of reasons arguments against privileging the Bible are increasingly heard. One notable example is Hector Avalos, who has argued strongly (albeit tendentiously) that "there is really nothing in the entire book Christians call 'the Bible' that is any more relevant than anything else written in the ancient world," and that the only worthwhile goal for future biblical studies should be to show "why human beings should never again privilege any book to this extent."[22] At least as far as study of the biblical texts within their ancient contexts goes (still the dominant mode of academic biblical scholarship), it is

---

[19]A classic modern account is William Wrede, "The Tasks and Methods of 'New Testament Theology,'" in Robert Morgan, *The Nature of New Testament Theology* (London: SCM, 1973), pp. 68-116.

[20]This is the general tenor of, for example, Francesca Stavrakopoulou and John Barton, eds., *Religious Diversity in Ancient Israel and Judah* (London and New York: T & T Clark, 2010).

[21]Andrew Louth, *Discerning the Mystery: An Essay on the Nature of Theology* (Oxford: Clarendon, 1983), p. 93.

[22]Hector Avalos, *The End of Biblical Studies* (Amherst, NY: Prometheus, 2007), pp. 22, 29.

hard to see how one can gainsay Avalos's basic point without making some appeal to postbiblical Jewish and Christian priorities. As Jon Levenson puts it:

> The very value-neutrality of this [historical-critical] method of study puts its practitioners at a loss to defend the *value* of the enterprise itself. In a culture saturated with religious belief involving the Bible, this weakness was less apparent, for the defense was less called for. Now, however, after secularism has impugned the worth of the Bible, and multiculturalism has begun to critique the cultural traditions at the base of which it stands, biblical scholars, including, I must stress, even the most antireligious among them, must face this paradoxical reality: the vitality of their rather untraditional discipline has historically depended upon the vitality of traditional religious communities, Jewish and Christian. Those . . . scholars who assiduously place the Bible in the ancient Near Eastern or Greco-Roman worlds . . . have depended for their livelihood upon those who not only rejoice that the Bible survived those worlds but who also insist that it deserved to survive because its message is transhistorical.[23]

In short, *canon* embodies major and contested value judgments about the biblical documents and their content, judgments that make a difference to the frame of reference within which Christian interpreters work and to the hermeneutical challenges they face.

Canon and hermeneutical expectations. Thirdly, the concept of canon relates to the *expectations that one may appropriately bring to the reading of the Bible,* especially in relation to the deity. It is striking, for example, how many scholars, including those who insist that the scholar should go where the evidence leads, untrammeled by ecclesial expectations, nonetheless expect to find truth about God and humanity in the Bible; and they do not linger to justify this or reflect on why they do not

---

[23]Levenson, "Historical Criticism," pp. 109-10.

bring the same expectations to other texts.[24] Of course, this is because they are Christians, or influenced by Christianity. But what difference should this make to their work as scholars?

As elsewhere, appreciation of the point can be enhanced by pondering its denial. Richard Dawkins makes the point with characteristic zest:

> I have found it an amusing strategy, when asked whether I am an atheist, to point out that the questioner is also an atheist when considering Zeus, Apollo, Amon Ra, Mithras, Baal, Thor . . . I just go one god further.
>
> All of us feel entitled to express extreme skepticism to the point of outright disbelief—except that in the case of unicorns, tooth fairies and the gods of Greece, Rome, Egypt and the Vikings, there is (nowadays) no need to bother. In the case of the Abrahamic God, however, there is a need to bother, because a substantial proportion of the people with whom we share the planet do believe strongly in his existence.[25]

In contrast to this, Brevard Childs, speaking as a Christian, says:

> I do not come to the Old Testament to learn about someone else's God, but about the God we confess, who has made himself known to Israel, to Abraham, Isaac and to Jacob. I do not approach some ancient concept, some mythological construct akin to Zeus or Moloch, but our God, our Father. The Old Testament bears witness that God revealed himself to Abraham, and we confess that he has broken into our lives. I do not come to the Old Testament to be informed about some strange religious phenomenon, but in faith I strive for knowledge as I seek to understand ourselves in the light of God's self-disclosure. In the context of the church's scripture I seek to be pointed to our God who has

---

[24]I have discussed this more fully in my "Theological Interpretation, Presuppositions, and the Role of the Church: Bultmann and Augustine Revisited," *Journal of Theological Interpretation* 6, no. 1 (2012): 1-22.

[25]Richard Dawkins, *The God Delusion* (London: Bantam, 2006), pp. 53-54.

made himself known, is making himself known, and will make himself known.[26]

This issue is nicely focused in the increasing number of scholars who quite reasonably query the convention of referring to the biblical deity as "God" (uppercase) rather than "god" (lowercase). In neither Hebrew nor Greek manuscripts from antiquity is the biblical deity distinguished from others by such capitalizing (though there are of course other conventions, related to the tetragrammaton in Hebrew texts and the *nomina sacra* in Greek texts), and so it is a convention dependent upon Jewish and Christian presuppositions about the reality and identity of the God of whom the Bible speaks.

In short, *canon* implies a belief that there is fundamental, though contested, truth about ultimate reality that is expressed in the biblical documents. Such a belief surely cannot but make a difference to the way Christian biblical interpreters approach their task.

Canon and the quest to clarify truth claims about God and humanity. A fourth facet of the biblical canon is the expectation not only that truth about God and humanity is present in the Bible but also that *biblical study should engage and clarify the nature and meaning of that truth.* The issue is nicely posed by Rex Mason's account of his activity as a Christian Old Testament scholar only fifteen years ago:

> Strictly speaking, it is the Old Testament scholar's brief to try to explain as well as he or she can just what he thinks the biblical author is saying. When that is done he or she can bow off the stage in thankful anonymity, concealed in a smokescreen of objectivity. If we go on to ask, "Does what the biblical writer is saying here make any sense?," or "Is there any way it can possibly be relevant or even 'true' for later times?," the scholar is no more equipped than anyone else to answer.[27]

---

[26]Brevard S. Childs, *Old Testament Theology in a Canonical Context* (London: SCM, 1985), pp. 28-29.
[27]Rex Mason, *Propaganda and Subversion in the Old Testament* (London: SPCK, 1997), pp. 107-8.

To be sure, it is doubtful that such an account of the biblical scholar's task would have commanded the assent of most of the giants of twentieth-century biblical scholarship: say, Walther Eichrodt and Gerhard von Rad in Old Testament, or Rudolph Bultmann and Ernst Käsemann in New Testament. Nevertheless, the suggestion by a respected mainstream English biblical scholar that substantive questions of biblical truth apparently either do not matter, or lack criteria by which they can appropriately be discussed by scholars as scholars, is surely startling.

In this context, ideologically suspicious approaches can be valuable in constraining the Christian scholar to (re-)engage with hard questions about the truth, or otherwise, of biblical content. David Clines raises the issue with characteristic vigor:

> The practitioners of the historical-critical method, like the inventors of the atomic bomb, were ethically irresponsible. Their commitment was to the "truth," whatever that might be and wherever it might lead. And that is unquestionably a whole sight better than a commitment to falsity. But it systematically ignored the question of effects on readers, and it is about time we regarded such study as part of our scholarly discipline and task....
>
> To be truly academic, and worthy of its place in the academy, biblical studies has to be truly critical, critical not just about lower-order questions like the authorship of the biblical books or the historicity of the biblical narratives, but critical about the Bible's contents, its theology, its ideology. And that is what biblical studies has notoriously not been critical about at all.[28]

For Clines this means that interpreters should position themselves outside the ideology of the biblical writers, and should as a matter of

---

[28]David J. A. Clines, "Why Is There a Song of Songs and What Does It Do to You If You Read It?" in his *Interested Parties: The Ideology of Writers and Readers of the Hebrew Bible*, Journal for the Study of the Old Testament Supplement Series 205 (Sheffield, UK: Sheffield Academic, 1995), pp. 107, 109. It is a moot point whether this is an accurate depiction of mainstream biblical studies.

course read against the grain of the biblical text. Christian interpreters, who will in general attach greater importance to reading with the grain, need nonetheless to take the challenge seriously. If for Christians the heart of the Bible is Jesus Christ as the one who definitively shows the true nature both of God and of human life, and if in his life, death and resurrection he overturns conventional human understandings of power and priorities, then the Bible contains a critique of culture and church more searching than any other because it represents ultimate reality.

Thus ideological suspicion gives opportunity for Christian scholars genuinely to re-engage the subject matter of those texts held to be canonical, and the all-important question of the impact of biblical content on human life.

Canon and recontextualization. A fifth aspect of the canon is that it directs attention to *the importance of recontextualization.* The content of the biblical documents has remained meaningful and authoritative, even as they have been interpreted and used in countless contexts other than their contexts of origin. Although, to be sure, it has sometimes been held that the history of biblical interpretation is essentially a history of misinterpretation, of texts being taken to mean something other than what they really mean (which is established only by relocating them in the originating frame of reference),[29] such an approach in effect denies that texts should be able to function in the way that scriptural texts do; but it is hardly obvious why such a denial should be plausible. As with classics such as Shakespeare's plays, we are unlikely to engage the plays with exactly the same mindset as Shakespeare himself or his initial Elizabethan and Jacobean audiences (although of course we can do our homework to try better to enter into the thought-world of that time), and so we may well not understand his plays in their "original" sense. But this does not mean that we misunderstand them (though of course in particular ways

---

[29]A remarkable nineteenth-century account along such lines is Frederic W. Farrar, *History of Interpretation* (London: Macmillan, 1886). For a recent variation on this theme, see Robin Lane Fox, *The Unauthorized Version: Truth and Fiction in the Bible* (London: Viking, 1991).

we might), but rather that their content has enduring power to engage people in different times and places.

The very process of preserving and collating material within a scriptural collection means that recontextualization features already within the biblical canon. This can sometimes be extensive, as with the Pentateuch or many of the Psalms where material has been written, preserved, combined with other writings and regarded as significant for subsequent generations. Indeed, one can include under the heading of recontextualization the two-testament nature of the Bible, and the fact that Israel's Scriptures become the Old Testament when they are read in conjunction with the New Testament. As such, these pre-Christian texts need to be read Christianly. What this involves is of course contested (I understand it to involve reading the text with dialectical attentiveness to at least four frames of reference: pre-Christian, Christian, Jewish and secular). Another way of putting the general point is that while modern biblical study has generally worked with an "author-hermeneutic," canonical documents require also a "text-hermeneutic" that is open to considering what a text may validly mean beyond the concerns of its author.[30]

Jon Levenson has interestingly, and surely rightly, argued that the plurality of contexts within which Scripture is read provides a way of rearticulating the ancient and medieval understanding that Scripture has more than one sense:

> Just as in medieval Europe there could be interreligious agreement on the *sensus literalis*, so in modern biblical criticism there will continue to be a broad base for agreement on the meaning of textual units in their most limited literary or historical settings. But when we come to "the final literary setting" and even more so to "the context of the canon," we [sc. Jews and Christians] must part company, for *there is no non-particularistic access to these larger*

---

[30]See, e.g., Luis Alonso Schökel, *A Manual of Hermeneutics* (Sheffield, UK: Sheffield Academic Press, 1998).

contexts, and no decision on these issues, even when made for secular purposes, can be neutral between Judaism and Christianity. Jews and Christians can, of course, study each other's Bible and even identify analogically or empathetically with the interpretations that the other's traditional context warrants, growing in discernment and self-understanding as a consequence. For the normative theological task, however, a choice must be made: Does the canonical context of the Abraham story, for example, include the Abraham material in Galatians and Romans or not? For Christians it must; for Jews it must not.[31]

Or, in a related formulation:

In the realm of historical criticism, pleas for a "Jewish biblical scholarship" or a "Christian biblical scholarship" are senseless and reactionary. Practicing Jews and Christians will differ from uncompromising historicists, however, in affirming the meaningfulness and interpretive relevance of larger contexts that homogenize the literatures of different periods to one degree or another. Just as text has more than one context, and biblical studies more than one method, so scripture has more than one sense, as the medievals knew and Tyndale, Spinoza, Jowett, and most other moderns have forgotten.[32]

Thus the canonical status of the biblical documents requires that Christian biblical interpreters be able to read the text in more than one context, and be able to articulate criteria for reading the text well that move beyond, even while they do not neglect, its likely meaning in its context of origin.

Canon and authoritative interpretation. The privileging of the bib-

[31]Jon Levenson, "The Eighth Principle of Judaism and the Literary Simultaneity of Scripture," in his *The Hebrew Bible, the Old Testament, and Historical Criticism: Jews and Christians in Biblical Studies* (Louisville: Westminster John Knox, 1993), pp. 80-81.

[32]Levenson, "Theological Consensus or Historicist Evasion? Jews and Christians in Biblical Studies," in *Hebrew Bible,* p. 104.

lical documents for the life and thought of the church means that *various authoritative interpretations are necessary,* so that these documents which have great diversity both of form and of content can be meaningfully appropriated. Authoritative interpretation takes a variety of forms. The creeds are summaries of the content of Christian faith, derived from Scripture, which are meant to play back on and structure a reading of Scripture.[33] Likewise, the notion of a rule of faith is surely inescapable. To have a rule of faith means, in essence, to have a big picture of how things go within a Christian frame of reference, a picture that is brought to bear heuristically on biblical reading, such that one can see the wood as well as the trees.

Of course, to speak about authoritative interpretation, creeds and a rule of faith can set alarm bells ringing for some. For is not this to surrender the freedom of the scholar to the constraints of ecclesial authority?[34] This objection is not to be taken lightly, for there are too many dismaying examples of heavy-handed censorship in the history of Protestant and Catholic churches, and more recently Orthodox churches; denominational seminaries and institutionally confessional university theology departments can sometimes be uncomfortable and unhealthy places for biblical study. But, as ever, abuse does not remove right use. The point of a rule of faith, and related notions, is not to deny that the Bible can legitimately be read for purposes other than those of faith, or to preempt the question of how what Scripture says is best understood if the plain sense of the text appears to be at odds with traditional ecclesial formulations or with Christian moral values. Rather, one primary point of a rule of faith is the need to have a picture and construal of biblical content as a whole—which, given the diversity and complexity of biblical content, is no easy matter.

---

[33]The relative silence about the Old Testament in the creeds—nothing about God's call of Abraham or Moses, or about God's forming and calling Israel to serve him—means that there is a significant hermeneutical deficit, which may to some extent express and may have further facilitated historic Christian distance from the Jewish people.

[34]For a fuller discussion of this issue, see my "Biblical Criticism and Religious Belief."

Moreover, a rule of faith also relates to the inherent difficulty of speaking truly about God. As I have put it elsewhere:

> On the one hand, the initial concern [sc. of a rule of faith] is not so much to explain the Bible at all (in senses familiar to philologist or historian) as to preserve its reality as authoritative and canonical for subsequent generations, so that engagement with the God of whom it speaks, and the transformations of human life which it envisages, remain enduring possibilities; that is, to say "God is here." On the other hand, the interest is not so much the history of ideas and religious practices (though this remains an important critical control) as the necessities of hermeneutics and theology proper, that is, the question of what is necessary to enable succeeding generations of faithful, or would-be faithful, readers to penetrate and grasp the meaning and significance of the biblical text; that is, to say "God is here" in such a way that the words can be rightly understood without lapse into idolatry, literalism, bad history, manipulation, or the numerous other pitfalls into which faith may stumble. It is when the Christian community fails sufficiently to grasp the implications of its own foundational text that a rule of faith changes role from guide to inquisitor.[35]

It is appropriate also to mention the role of particular figures in the life of the church down the ages who have offered large-scale construals of Scripture as a whole that have helped make Scripture widely comprehensible—I think of the role that Origen and Augustine played in antiquity, and that Luther and Calvin played for the churches of the Reformation (which has meant that particular overall ways of reading the text have been adopted by many in the churches who may not have known where their pattern of reading originated). Such figures provide particular frames of reference, or paradigms, for the reading of Scripture,

---

[35]R. Walter Moberly, *The Bible, Theology, and Faith* (Cambridge: Cambridge University Press, 2000), p. 43.

which can have a long-term vitality and fruitfulness.[36]

Under this general heading it is worth mentioning the general point that, because the canonical documents are so important within the life of the church, the church has traditionally recognized the importance of specialized activities of scholarship and teaching to complement and support the church's engagement with these documents. There is much within Scripture that is difficult to understand; and there is much that, whether or not intrinsically difficult, is easily misunderstood. And, as already noted, there are demanding questions about how to understand and appropriate the truth of Scripture. Although, sadly, many in the churches are indifferent, or even hostile, to the work of biblical scholarship, it remains an indispensable corollary of Scripture's authoritative role.

The professional biblical scholar should also not forget the enormous impact of those who can communicate in the life of the church beyond the academy—a parable of which may be the fact that C. S. Lewis is unmentioned in David Ford's compendious guide to modern theologians,[37] even though Lewis's popular theological writings have arguably been more widely read, and been more influential in the churches, than those of any of the figures who are included in Ford's book.[38]

Canon and Christian identity and practice. One final issue, implicit in what has already been said yet meriting explicit mention, is *the role of canonical scripture in forming Christian identity and life practices.* On the

---

[36]A fascinating analogy can be seen in the enduring influence upon Americans of Abraham Lincoln's reading of the foundational constitutional documents of American life, even while his reading in important ways clearly differs from the original sense of the documents. See Gary Wills, *Lincoln at Gettysburg: The Words That Remade America* (New York: Simon & Schuster, 1992), esp. pp. 38-39, 147.

[37]David F. Ford and Rachel Muers, eds., *The Modern Theologians: An Introduction to Christian Theology Since 1918*, 3rd ed. (Malden, MA: Blackwell, 2005).

[38]It is worth asking who the influential interpreters of Scripture are at the present (at least, in English-speaking contexts). Perhaps, among others, Walter Brueggemann and John Goldingay for the Old Testament, and Tom Wright and Luke Johnson for the New Testament? This would be not least because they all speak and write extensively both for academic and for ecclesial and nonspecialist audiences.

one hand, there is the role of Scripture in Christian worship. Liturgies are often extensively fashioned out of scriptural content (with selections and renderings that are hermeneutically complex), and Scripture is also read in worship. Indeed, because Scripture is foundational for Christian identity, it is privileged in worship as no other text is or can be: whatever else *may* be read, Scripture *must* be read.

On the other hand, a healthy rediscovery in recent hermeneutics is that patterns and practices of living can constitute a good way of rendering the meaning of the biblical text. As Nicholas Lash has so well put it:

> The practice of Christian faith is not, in the last resort, a matter of interpreting, in our time and place, an ancient text. It is, or seeks to be, the faithful "rendering" of those events, of those patterns of human action, decision and suffering, to which the texts bear original witness. To acknowledge that the criteria of fidelity are hard to establish and are frequently problematic is to admit that there is, indeed, a hermeneutical "gap." But this "gap" does not lie, in the last resort, between what was once "meant" and what might be "meant" today. It lies, rather, between what was once achieved, intended, or "shown," and what might be achieved, intended, or "shown" today.[39]

To suggest that (to put the point strongly) the saints, both ancient and modern, may be exemplary interpreters of Scripture is not to polarize piety and reason and so denigrate the numerous mundane intellectual disciplines that the regular biblical scholar needs to master. Rather it is a reminder both of the wider purposes that the disciplined interpretation of Scripture should serve and of the way in which concerns as to how life should be lived appropriately impact biblical

---

[39]Nicholas Lash, "What Might Martyrdom Mean?" in his *Theology on the Way to Emmaus* (London: SCM, 1986), pp. 90-91; repr. from W. Horbury and B. McNeill, eds., *Suffering and Martyrdom in the New Testament* (Cambridge: Cambridge University Press, 1981), pp. 183-98. More generally, see Stephen Barton, "New Testament Interpretation as Performance," in his *Life Together: Family, Sexuality and Community in the New Testament and Today* (Edinburgh: T & T Clark, 2001), pp. 223-50.

hermeneutics. Scholarly debates in this general area abound—contemporary feminist, liberation or ecological concerns come readily to mind—but the underlying concern for the reintegration of thought and life in relation to making sense of Scripture is the important point for our present concern.

Conclusions

Three remarks in conclusion.

First, nothing I have said should be taken to deny that there are valid ways of reading the Bible other than as Christian Scripture. Israel's Scriptures and the documents of the early church can undoubtedly be studied as interesting expressions of life and thought in antiquity, with no assumption of their enduring significance. Likewise the Bible can be studied as a cultural classic, of historic and continuing influence in Western civilization, again with no assumption of its enduring truth-content concerning God or humanity. But there is a real question as to whether the best locations for such studies might not be departments of ancient history and cultural studies, rather than theology, despite theology's interests in the results of such studies. How biblical interpreters who acknowledge ecclesial responsibility should best interrelate with those who operate without such a frame of reference is an ongoing challenge, probably best worked out less in the abstract than in the discussion of specific readings of the biblical text and of the purposes that they serve.

Secondly, if my thick account of ecclesial responsibility is on the right lines in terms of all the issues of which the Christian biblical interpreter should be aware and should take into account, then one may well ask: Who is sufficient for these things? Contemporary academic life tends to pressure scholars to narrow rather than expand their intellectual focus. One might be tempted to wish that it really were as simple as supposing that the alternative to unconstrained philological and historical investigation were to "feed the churches with 'edifying' or 'reverent' scholarship," rather than try to clarify the nature of the truth content of the

Bible's account of God and humanity, and its possible appropriation, over against other construals of life in the world. We surely need some major rethinking of the shape and content of the theological curriculum (the note on which Dale Martin's critique of contemporary American theological education ended).

Finally, how do I think about the Pastorals some thirty-five years later? In terms of authorship, I am agnostic: the distinctiveness of tone and content in relation to the undisputed Pauline letters is not in doubt, but arguments as to how best to account for this in terms of origins are inconclusive. However, the authority of the letters is secured not by their authorship as such, but by their canonical status, historic reception and historic fruitfulness. If Paul in the Pastorals has undergone an interpretative process somewhat analogous to that of Jesus in John's Gospel, then I take the fruit of that process as a witness to the multifaceted depth of its subject matter. In any event, literary theory makes it possible to take the first-person voice of the letters with full imaginative seriousness, and one can unreservedly inhabit the imaginative world of the text in preaching, while leaving open the relation between literary voice and historical author. As I compare the hermeneutical resources that are available now with those that were available then, I am grateful that real progress has been made.

Conclusion

Remaining Hermeneutical Issues for the Future of Biblical Interpretation

Stanley E. Porter and Matthew R. Malcolm

THE VARIED VOICES HAVE SPOKEN. What now can we observe and learn from this panoply of hermeneutical approaches?

The contributors themselves represent a relatively narrow range of scholarly and intellectual backgrounds. Most of them are biblical scholars of the Old and/or New Testaments, as we might expect. One or two would probably consider themselves primarily theologians, as is also appropriate. However, despite this fairly confined range of backgrounds, the questions they pose, the analyses they present and the suggestions they offer regarding the future of biblical interpretation certainly indicate responsible plurality, but not necessarily the plurality that one might expect. By that we mean that, apart from the contribution of Professor Thiselton's chapter and perhaps a few others, plurality is found more in the aggregate whole of the contributions than it is in the individual parts of their individual offerings. Rather than there being a sustained argument for responsible hermeneutical plurality across the range of issues, there is instead a kind of individualized hermeneutical univocity within each of several of the papers. This is a univocity distinctly different in most respects from the univocity of each of the other individual contributors, hence its only being able to be seen to constitute a hermeneutical plurality in the aggregate. In other words, rather than each, or even most, of the contributors settling on a kind of responsible plurality in hermeneutics as the way forward in biblical interpretation, many if not most of the contributors have ended up arguing for their type of individual hermeneutics, as a legitimate and necessary means of defining and settling the major issues in hermeneutics.

On the one hand, we suppose that such an outcome is entirely to be expected. The contributors to this volume are, each in his own way, accomplished and highly regarded academics with areas of recognized research and specialization, and they were asked to engage specific areas within hermeneutics. One would expect them to write and contribute within their areas of expertise and competence, and so they have. On the other hand, the very nature of hermeneutics, and certainly as it has been demonstrated in the work of Professor Thiselton, is to push interpreters beyond their areas of intellectual and academic comfort, to force them to recognize—if not embrace—the other in interpretation, to the point of expanding their own intellectual and interpretive boundaries and being able to constructively engage with new horizons of understanding. Perhaps that is asking too much, although when we survey the results of these individual efforts we do find in the whole more than simply the sum of the individual parts. In the composite, we have learned much more about hermeneutics and the issues that it must face in order to confront and shape a constructive future for biblical interpretation.

What are these major issues in hermeneutics that need to be solved? We see four of them as particularly germane. These include: the fundamental question of the definition of what hermeneutics is, the role of the Bible and in particular the New Testament in the larger hermeneutical endeavor, the locus of hermeneutical authority, and the role of tradition or the church in hermeneutics. Each of these merits further discussion.

The fundamental question in hermeneutics, even or especially at the end of this volume, is the question of what in fact is hermeneutics. According to our contributors, there are at least two particular strands to this question. The first strand or element of discussion is the relationship of hermeneutics to interpretation, and the other is whether hermeneutics is concerned with or focused upon ancient meaning, modern meaning or some combination of them, and, if so, in what proportions. A good example of the tension is found within the contrasting emphases of the papers by James Dunn and Robert Morgan. Dunn, a New Testament scholar, sees a very close association between hermeneutics and interpretation, in that whatever it is that is being done in the hermeneutical exercise is to be related to or in direct service of interpretation of the biblical text. Hermeneutics for Dunn, in other words, is the study of the principles of interpretation, rather than a more abstract consideration of the nature of human understanding. More particularly, Dunn not only answers the question of what hermeneutics is by apparently advocating for the priority of interpretation, but he sees the horizon of the original author in his or her historical situation as the key determining or limiting factor in the activity of interpretation. This is not to say that Dunn holds it to be the only limiting factor; nevertheless his emphasis on the horizon of the original author may lead some to consider him an advocate for a single-meaning interpretive framework.[1] Many will notice similarity to the approach advocated by the literary scholar and cultural critic E. D. Hirsch, even if Dunn does not frame the issues in quite the same way. By contrast, Robert Morgan, also a New Testament scholar but with extensive interpretive interests, frames hermeneutics within a critical theological framework, in which there is a constant interaction between the ancient text and the modern inter-

---

[1]It should not be thought that Dunn necessarily holds this horizon of the original author to directly govern contemporary theology or practice. For Dunn, texts may well be relativized for contemporary application, but the point is that this relativization involves the key consideration of attention to historical circumstance, allowing distance between the text's historical "meaning" and present-day belief or practice.

preter—the classic formulation of the two horizons—that not only must be recognized but constitutes the essential framework of human understanding. Rather than opting for a Barthian formulation, which is all too common in recent hermeneutical discussion, Morgan wishes to draw upon Bultmann's critical theological approach, in which the historical and theological issues are and remain in tension.

In some ways, Dunn's approach is probably more typical for biblical scholars, who wish to find a solid foundation upon which to stand as the basis of their interpretation, so that, even if they do not wish to normalize their findings, they have a secure sense of what the text *says* because they are confident of what it *said*. That is, they parse the then–now distinction in terms of then having priority over now. Morgan, however, believes that modern critical theology must in some cases even trump the ancient text, especially when it speaks of things that are unacceptable to modern interpreters. In these two essays alone, we see that the question of what hermeneutics is can (still) be answered in radically different ways. Dunn essentially wishes to circumvent or even bracket out many of the major issues in the last several hundred years of hermeneutical discussion in order to firmly reassert the historical foundations of the biblical text. This is completely understandable in the light of the traditional historical stance and foundations of Christianity. Morgan essentially wishes to embrace these developments, even if they are at the expense of textual continuity in support of theological enhancement and relevance. Allied with this debate is the question of where biblical hermeneutics fits within the areas of general and special hermeneutics. Stanley Porter and Matthew Malcolm, New Testament scholars with wide hermeneutical interests, both look at biblical hermeneutics within the wider sphere of general hermeneutics. For them, biblical hermeneutics, or rather hermeneutics that is focused upon the Bible, is not a special type of hermeneutics, but it is a type or even subcategory of general hermeneutics that is directed at the Bible, with all of the attendant issues that come about as a result. Porter goes even further and wishes to affirm the ability to hold the tension of original and contemporary meaning in constructive opposition, on the basis of the realization that, if properly formulated, hermeneutics is about contemporary meaning but on the basis of meaning in the past.

For virtually all of the essays in this volume, the Bible is not too far away from the forefront of discussion. Rightly so, as Professor Thiselton is first and foremost an outstanding New Testament interpreter. In some of the essays of this volume, the Bible looms larger than others, but in all of them, whether the formulation is directly made in terms of specific texts or more generally couched in a regard for Christian theology, the Bible has an important role to play. However, that role is significantly different from essay to essay. There is a tension within the essays concerning whether the Bible is a collection of individual texts, some of them potentially highly problematic to interpret and contemporaneously apply, or whether the Bible is less a historical document than it is a canonical or theological document. In these essays at least, those who approach the Bible as a collection of individual texts seem for the most part to accept many of the so-called assured results of critical scholarship. It is not always explicitly stated whether these critical conclusions are on the basis of the kind of approach that is being advocated towards hermeneutics, or whether these critical results constitute the basis of the hermeneutical problem that must be solved by the particular advocate's hermeneutical stance. Walter Moberly, an Old Testament scholar with wide-ranging interests, begins his essay with the well-known problem of authorship of the Pastoral Epistles and the potential dilemma this poses when one wishes to proclaim the Word of God—especially if they are not even the words of Paul but someone who is writing in Paul's name, whether for noble or ignoble purposes. Richard Briggs, a hermeneut who specializes in the Bible, extends the notion of the Bible by reformulating it in terms not of *Scripture is* but of *Scripture as*. The first move he makes is reconceptualizing the Bible not as a collection of books or even as a single book but as Scripture. *Scripture* implies an entire hermeneutical framework of what one thinks of this document that stands at the center of Christian faith. Reconceptualizing it in terms of "Scripture as" allows one to explore the various ways that Scripture functions. So, Scripture may function as text, as bearer of meaning, as some type of functional communication, or, in the extreme, as one's own construal of function or meaning. Briggs pulls back from the last and wishes to see Scripture as in conversation with itself. In a sense, Briggs abandons the notion of Scripture and reverts to a pluriform textuality, in which the Bible is a series of dialogical texts. There is a distinct sense within the several essays of this volume that the Bible is at one and the same time and in varying ways both a bounded and an unbounded set. It is a bounded set in that it is a text or a series of texts, situated in time and place. However, it is also an unbounded set in that it functions within a much wider sphere. It is read and interpreted in the present, is seen to convey meaning not only to the original readers but to modern interpreters (sometimes apparently even different meanings from those conveyed to the original readers), and is thought to have meaning that in fact transcends these boundaries and provides for open-ended meaning—if rightly and responsibly interpreted.

If this is the case, such that even for a reader such as Dunn there is more to the Bible than simply its situational specificity, what then constitutes the ground of authority for its interpretation? What is the center of interpretative authority? There are both micro- and macro-interpretative parameters suggested by our various hermeneutical scholars. Matthew Malcolm finds hermeneutical authority in structures within the biblical text itself, such as patterns of kerygma. He formulates this as kerygmatic responsibility. At the same time, he admits that the kerygmatic patterns vary within the New Testament, but that these are a means of controlling the interpretative possibilities of an open-ended text such as the Bible (being open-ended is, for him, a good thing, although it needs to be moderated). Moberly sees authority in ecclesial responsibility, which he in effect interprets as the canonical text as endorsed by the church. In fact, for Moberly, the canon—even if there are recognizable problems with its formulation and history (to the point of recognizing several canons, or at least two canonical Old Testaments, the Greek and the Hebrew, as he stated during questions after his paper)—solves all of the major problems of interpretative authority (or at least suggests their resolution). These include questions regarding how disparate documents can be interpreted together, setting the boundaries of legitimate interpretation, allowing for what he calls recontextualization, and forming the basis for Christian life and practice. Tom Greggs, a systematic theologian, sees the creeds and early symbols of the church as providing the grounds of authoritative interpretation. This is the most far-reaching proposal offered in this volume in that it departs the furthest from the biblical text itself, although Greggs is careful to want to ensure that he places Scripture as having priority over the creeds. The creeds and symbols of the early church are definitive and authoritative examples and instances of what he calls *relational responsibility*, and hence function as a means of affirming the principle of *sola scriptura*.

As for the role of the church and tradition in hermeneutics, as we have already indicated in discussion of interpretative authority, for most of the contributors to this volume the church and tradition play an important role in creating hermeneutical responsibility—even if they often formulate it differently. For Dunn, this means attention to the historical groundedness of the biblical documents, which ends up being a theologically responsible affirmation of incarnation, while for Morgan it means attention to theological responsibility, even if it must be critical. For Malcolm, the role of tradition is formulated within the biblical documents themselves, and then it pervades and constrains their subsequent interpretation as open texts. For Briggs, Moberly and Greggs, though each in different ways, the church is instrumental in constituting the means of arbitrating the potentially conflicting legitimacy of theological interpretation. This means that whether one is speaking of a functional interpretation of Scripture within the church, or of the role of canon in defining the parameters of legitimate interpretation, or of the creeds and tradition as constituting the relational responsibility necessary for biblical interpretation, the church and tradition are fundamental to legitimate hermeneutical endeavor. Porter does not necessarily disagree with this, although as perhaps the cautious voice in the mix he warns that theological hermeneutics needs to distinguish itself from so-called theological interpretation, a recent movement within Christian theology and biblical interpretation. Theological interpretation of Scripture, as it is usually formulated and practiced, tends toward distinguishing itself from theological hermeneutics. This is seen in its move toward becoming a method of interpretation in its own right, its in some ways nonhermeneutical stance, and its ambiguous and potentially unhelpful approach to early church tradition. Christian tradition and the church cannot play the kind of role that they need to play in biblical hermeneutics if they are used as tools to manipulate acts of interpretation, rather than serving as fostering responsible plurality in interpretation.

To this point, we have not said anything specifically about Professor Thiselton's chapter. It is difficult for us to respond to this chapter, for a number of reasons. One of these is that the authors of this chapter, as well as virtually all of the participants in the conference that prompted this volume, owe so much to his fundamental work in the area of hermeneutics that it is difficult for us to try to position ourselves in relationship to his seminal thinking. Most of the (good) ideas that most of us have are in one way or another the products of his earlier and continuing work, to the point where in many instances it is difficult to know whether some of our ideas are genuinely ours or whether they are Professor Thiselton's deeply embedded in our own thinking due to his foundational influence upon us. Another reason is that we willingly recognize that Professor Thiselton has carved out a unique place for himself within the field of hermeneutics, including biblical hermeneutics, and many of the questions that he asks are, at the heart of it, the fundamental questions that all of us should have been asking all along, though we often have not. As a result, we find that his chapter in itself advances the discussion in ways that perhaps none of the other chapters do. His chapter at times embraces the awkward and at other times rejects the appealing or at least alluring, in elegant ways unique to him and his experience. The chapters within the volume itself, in at least a few instances to be sure, show glimpses of insight and progressive thought that could and may well push the boundaries of the discipline forward. There is also, however, a sense in which all of these chapters, while trying to have one eye on the future, have (the metaphor is an unsettling one) another and perhaps a larger eye trained on the past. There is a sense in which many if not most of the chapters are attempts at self-justification of a particular approach to hermeneutics. This stance may be one advocated previously or it may be a more recent effort, but each is careful to position his attempt within this larger framework.

All of this is not to say that Professor Thiselton is not always careful to make clear the lines of connection between his ideas and those of his predecessors and his contemporaries. This he surely does. However, in his chapter, he also has not hesitated, even at this stage in his career, to push and encourage in new and progressive directions. He returns to the concept of the open text, not as a threat to determinative meanings, but as a recognition of the continuing challenge and possibilities of biblical hermeneutics and interpretation. Even though his position is not a popular one among contemporary interpreters, he once more argues for a two-level interpretation of Old Testament texts used in the New, consistent with his view of the plurivocity of the Bible and the need for responsible hermeneutics. He also makes abundantly clear—lest there be any doubt—that the Bible is not the proverbial wax nose that can be bent in any direction. Nevertheless, he also recognizes that the history of interpretation, as well as good philosophical and hermeneutical reasoning, finds it difficult to deny the polyphony and Bakhtinian dialogical nature of the Bible. Professor Thiselton insightfully recognizes that the idea of polyphony is often construed as contradiction, when that is simply not the case. The result is not contradiction, but continuing conversation, discussion and seeking after meaning. Within the parameters set by the Bible itself, there is a recognizable and legitimate expression of difference. This is a commendable definition of hermeneutics and, perhaps even more to the point, responsible Christian behavior.